Anglican Religious Communities Year Book 2000 / 2001

Published by **Canterbury Press Norwich**
a publishing imprint of Hymns Ancient & Modern Limited
(a registered charity)
St Mary's Works, St Mary's Plain, Norwich, Norfolk, NR3 3BH

ARCYB 2000/2001 published September 1999

The cover design is by Leigh Hurlock.

Original line drawings by Sister Elizabeth Farley OSC, excepting those on pages 70 & 111 which are by Sister Mary Julian Gough CHC.

A catalogue record for this book is available from the British Library.

ISBN 1-85311-319-0

Contents

Foreword

by
The Archbishop of York

I warmly welcome a second edition of the *Anglican Religious Communities Year Book.* International in its coverage, it shows clearly the Religious Life in many different provinces of the Anglican Communion and is an excellent resource for the Church.

There is a tremendous range in the way the Religious Life is being lived out in our own church as we begin the third millennium. Amidst their varied ministries and mission, what undergirds the common life is a commitment to prayer, to making space for meeting God. And not only for the enrichment of the spiritual lives of the individual members of the communities, but for all who come to share in the life as guests and retreatants, for those looking for healing and those simply looking for welcome rather than rejection.

In commending this book therefore, I want especially to thank all those members of the Religious communities, all those men and women who have heard God's call to them to follow him on this particular path to the Kingdom, brothers and sisters whose lives of commitment and prayer are a constant reminder to us all of what our faith is about.

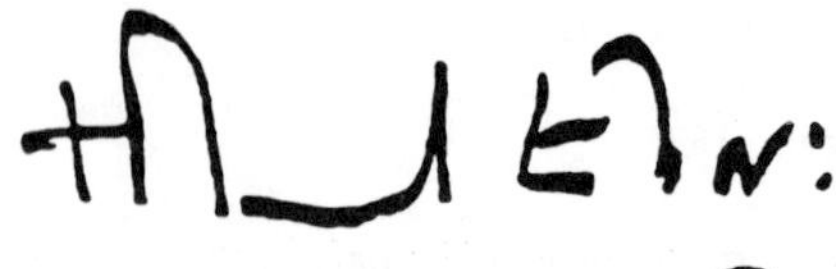

Day of Prayer for Vocations to the Religious Life

Setting a particular Sunday each year as a Day of Prayer for Vocations to the Religious Life was begun in 1992. This is currently The Fifth Sunday after Trinity, the collect for which is:

Almighty and everlasting God,
by whose Spirit
  the whole body of the Church
  is governed and sanctified:
hear our prayer
  which we offer for all your faithful people
that, in their vocation and ministry,
each may serve you in holiness and truth
  to the glory of your name;
through our Lord and Saviour Jesus Christ,
who is alive and reigns with you
  in the unity of the Holy Spirit,
one God,
now and for ever. Amen.

We give thanks for the Religious Life

1 Community of All Hallows *in the UK*
All Saints Sisters of the Poor *in the UK & the USA*
Society of the Precious Blood *in Lesotho, South Africa & the UK*
2 Community of the Holy Spirit *in the USA*
Community of St Mary *in the Philippines & the USA*
3 Community of the Resurrection *in South Africa & the UK*
Community of the Resurrection of Our Lord *in South Africa*
4 Community of Saint Francis & Society of Saint Francis *in Australia, New Zealand, Papua New Guinea, the Solomon Islands, the UK & the USA*
Korean Franciscan Brotherhood *in Korea*
Little Brothers of Francis *in Australia*
5 Community of the Servants of the Will of God *in the UK*
Community of the Servants of Jesus Christ *in Madagascar*
Society of the Franciscan Servants of Jesus & Mary *in the UK*
6 Community of the Epiphany *in the UK*
Sisterhood of the Epiphany *in India & the UK*
Christa Sevika Sangha *in Bangladesh*
Brotherhood of the Epiphany *in Bangladesh*
7 Community of Jesus' Compassion *in South Africa*
Community of the Holy Name *in Lesotho, South Africa, Swaziland & the UK*
8 Community of the Sisters of the Church *in Australia, Canada, the Solomon Islands & the UK*
Order of Julian of Norwich *in the USA*
9 Community of St Denys *in the UK*
Community of the Divine Compassion *in Zimbabwe*
Society of the Sacred Advent *in Australia*
10 Community of St Laurence *in the UK*
Chita Che Zita Renoyera (Holy Name Community) *in Zimbabwe; and* Chita Chezvipo Zvemoto (Community of the Gifts of the Holy Fire) *in Zimbabwe*
11 Order of St Benedict *in independent Abbeys and Priories in Australia, Korea, the UK & the USA*
Benedictine Community of the Holy Cross *in the UK*
Benedictine Community of Christ the King *in Australia*
12 Community of the Holy Transfiguration *in Zimbabwe*
Community of the Transfiguration *in the Dominican Republic & the USA*
13 Community of the Glorious Ascension *in France & the UK*
Brotherhood of the Ascended Christ *in India*
14 Community of the Servants of the Cross *in the UK*
Order of the Holy Cross *in Canada, South Africa & the USA*
Society of the Holy Cross *in Korea*
Society of the Sacred Cross *in the UK*
15 Community of St Mary the Virgin *in India, South Africa & the UK*
Society of Our Lady St Mary *in Canada*
Society of Our Lady of the Isles *in the UK*

in the Church, and today we pray for:

16 Order of the Teachers of the Children of God *in the USA*
Community of the Companions of Jesus the Good Shepherd *in the UK*
Community of the Good Shepherd *in Malaysia*
17 Melanesian Brotherhood *in Fiji, Papua New Guinea, the Philippines, the Solomon Islands & Vanuatu*
Community of the Sisters of Melanesia *in the Solomon Islands*
18 Oratory of the Good Shepherd *in South Africa, the UK & the USA*
Oblates & Tertiaries, Associates & Companions
19 Order of the Holy Paraclete *in Ghana, South Africa, Swaziland & the UK*
Community of the Holy Name *in Australia*
20 Society of St Margaret *in Haiti, Sri Lanka, the UK & the USA*
Ewell Monastery *in the UK*
21 Community of St Clare *in the UK*
The Clare Community *in Australia*
Order of St Helena *in the USA*
Community of Nazareth *in Japan*
22 Community of the Sacred Passion *in the UK*
Community of St Mary of Nazareth and Calvary *in Tanzania & Zambia*
23 Society of the Holy Trinity *in the UK*
Community of the Holy Family *in the UK*
Community of Reparation to Jesus in the Blessèd Sacrament *in the UK*
24 Community of St John Baptist *in the UK & the USA*
Community of St John the Baptist *in South Africa*
25 Community of St Paul *in Mozambique*
Society of St Paul *in the USA*
Sisterhood of the Holy Nativity *in the USA*
26 Order of St Anne *in the USA*
Community of the Sisters of the Love of God *in New Zealand & the UK*
27 Community of St John the Divine *in the UK*
Sisterhood of St John the Divine *in Canada*
Society of St John the Divine *in South Africa*
Community of St John the Evangelist *in the Republic of Ireland*
Society of St John the Evangelist *in the UK & the USA*
Sisters of Charity *in the UK & the USA*
28 Society of the Sacred Mission *in Australia, Lesotho, Papua New Guinea & the UK*
Sisters of the Incarnation *in Australia*
29 Community of St Michael & All Angels *in South Africa*
Community of St Peter *in Swaziland*
Community of St Peter (Woking) *in the UK*
Community of St Peter, Horbury *in the UK*
Society of the Sisters of Bethany *in the UK*
30 Community of St Andrew *in the UK*
Community of the Sacred Name *in Fiji & New Zealand*
31 Congregation of the Sisters of the Visitation of Our Lady *in Papua New Guinea*
Community of the Blessed Lady Mary *in Zimbabwe*

News of Anglican Religious Life

Anglican Religious Communities (ARC) in Europe

For many years, Anglican Religious Communities in the UK remained distinct and separate from each other, with (excepting formal occasions and superiors' meetings) few opportunities for members to meet each other. In the climate of renewal in the 1960s, however, several gatherings were organised for representatives to discuss the new challenges facing Religious Life. The first two meetings were held in Oxford in the 1960s, and out of a third, held in York in 1974, the Communities Consultative Council was created. Over the last twenty-five years, its structures have provided a place for discussion and the exchange of ideas, particularly at the annual conference.

However, for many Religious in recent years, the idea of a new structure has seemed more appropriate for the future - one which would bring the CCC together with the Leaders' Conference, the Novices' Conference and other inter-community organisations. Following a meeting of a small representative group on 8 October 1998, a recommendation was made to create a new body called Anglican Religious Communities (in Europe). It would have the acronym ARC. If this proposal is implemented, the ARC committee would be made up of representatives of the different groups: leaders, novice guardians, the Advisory Council and so on.

Consequently, in September 1999, a motion will be put to the CCC conference suggesting that the CCC as it now stands should be dissolved. An annual conference for community representatives would still be held, but as an opportunity to meet together rather than as a formal decision-making body with a constitution. If this motion is passed, ARC will then be created and the CCC's representative rôle and authority will pass to the new committee.

A Superior Team

The Order of St Helena in the USA has recently tried something different. Since 1997 it has not had a superior. Instead, with the backing of the whole community, an elected leadership council has shared responsibility. Each of the four members of the team has an area of administration or oversight for which she is responsible:

Sister Cintra is the administrative officer,
Sister Ellen Stephen is the President of Corporation,
Sister Rosina is minister of pastoral care,
Sister Linda Julian is minister of vocations.

Sharing the work of leadership has meant that each Sister elected to the Council has not had to give up her own on-going ministry.

The pattern has worked well so far. The Council meets every other month with a facilitator to deal with community business, with decisions being made by consensus instead of by votes.

Sister Bernardine CHN

Sister Bernardine CHN (Betty Stephenson) died on 24 December 1998. She was much loved and well-known to many who visited the Community of the Holy Name. Mother Jean Mary CHN writes about Sister's remarkable ministry:

She grew up in Brighton, and used to tell stories of the town during the Second World War, when the beaches were also a line of defences. She became a member of the congregation of St Peter's, Brighton, in her mid-teens, and was there at a time when they had a particularly flourishing and active youth club. Some of the relationships formed in that club have lasted to the present day, as we realised when former members, still in touch, came to visit Sister Bernardine when she was ill, and then attended her funeral. The club was a powerful influence.

Sister Bernardine came to CHN in 1964 and soon made her name as a cook of the first order. After profession in 1967, she became well-known working in the retreat houses at St Albans, and then, later, in Chester, where she ran the kitchen for ten years. Even sixteen years later, anyone who remembers her may well associate retreats with stocking up gastronomically as well as spiritually. People have continued to ask after her, including stall holders in the market as well as retreatants.

After a time in Malvern, Sister Bernardine went to Zambia, as there was a possiblity of helping to start a Zambian community. However, this venture did not in the end succeed, although she was a great support to those there and found living in Africa quite an adventure.

She came into her own when CHN moved to Derby and she became the Guest Sister. Many treasured her homely hospitality, her home cooking (again), her wit and her readiness to sit and listen. Welcoming guests with a cup of tea and a listening ear was a valuable service to those who came weary and tense. She will be greatly missed. The following poem written by one of those who valued all these gifts sums up so much of what she offered in that place. May she rest in peace.

It says of Bernardine,
Tidiness is valued.
For what she restores our
Fractured lives.
Not wanting to leave signs of
Disharmony in this security.
We wash and put away each tea-
spoon.
An act of unity of purpose,
A small communion.

(Ann R. Parker)

Healing and Peace

Healing the sick and providing a peaceful setting for retreatants have been ministries of the Community of All Hallows at Ditchingham for many years. Mother Sheila CAH writes with news of both:

Our hospital is being recognised as a provider of services for our local Primary Care Group (population: 107,000). Negotiations are progressing favourably between all those concerned, both with the administration and the care of the patients. In addition, a very generous donation from a local benefactor is allowing us to build a compact little extension, which will enhance and improve on the services already being offered.

Meanwhile, in response to guest questionnaires, health and safety requirements, building regulations and the perceived needs of users of our retreat and conference centres, St Gabriel's is (we hope) to undergo considerable extension, repair and refurbishment. This is scheduled for the end of 1999. We hope very much that both past and future users will regard the end result as comfortable, beautiful and restorative in the deepest sense of that word.

Golden Jubilee of CORL

On 13 October 1948, representatives of over twenty Anglican Religious communities in North America met for discussion. They wished to create an organisation which could both represent them to the Church and also bring their leaders together regularly to promote co-operation and contact. A year later, on 4 November 1949 at the parish house of St Mary the Virgin, New York, the group adopted a constitution. The Conference on the Religious Life in the Anglican Communion in the Americas had come into being. In its Golden Jubilee year, it remains an important forum for the exchange of ideas, bringing the leaders together for an annual conference. More about CORL can be found at its web site:

http://www.wthree.com/corl/

as well as on page 19 in this *Year Book*.

New Leaders

Several elections took place soon after the last edition of the *Year Book* went to press. Sister Judith succeeded Sister Janet in May 1998 as Prioress of the Order of the Holy Paraclete; and the following July, Sister Mary Jean was elected Mother of the Society of the Sacred Cross at Tymawr. In South Africa, Mother Carol was chosen in November 1998 to succeed Mother Nonie as leader of the Community of the Resurrection of Our Lord. Readers should be aware of two further elections in the Summer of 1999: one at the Community of the Sacred Passion in the UK and the other in Africa at the Community of St Mary of Nazareth and Calvary.

Labyrinthine Meditation

The Sisters of the Community of St Mary in Wisconsin have completed a very special place of meditation at their retreat house, Mary's Margin, at Wukmonago. They have created a walk in the form of a labyrinth, which is about a mile long and takes twenty minutes or more each way to complete. All visitors are welcome to do this spiritual exercise - not only those in retreat. Going on this meditative walk has become a daily feature of the Sisters' prayer-life. Sister Letitia writes:

Most labyrinths are geometric; they follow regular curves, crossing and spiraling within a set space. Ours is an organic labyrinth, following the shape of the land, winding through the trees, meandering down hills and across small meadows. It spirals in and out of the woods, crossing itself several times and covering virtually all of our five acres. At its heart, you're invited to climb high into a wooden prayer tower where you can see marsh, meadow, trees and hills flowing into limitless sky...

For those disinclined to climb, a hammock beckons. There you can contemplate chipmunks, scurrying squirrels, and the changing colors of the earth. No two labyrinth walks are ever the same. The trees, the light and the earth change constantly. ... As you consider the "lilies of the field", the truth of God's beauty can set you free.

New Community

The 19th of December 1998 was an important date in the life of one of the Anglican Communion's newest Religious communities. For it was on that day that seven sisters of the Community of Jesus' Compassion in South Africa took the community's first life professions. In addition, six novices took their first vows. The foundress of the community, Sister Londiwe, began her Religious Life as a sister in the Community of the Holy Name in Zululand, and began the foundation of CJC in the early 1990s. The main work of the community is evangelism in the area where they have settled, New Hanover, near Pietermaritzburg.

Sister Londiwe CJC

Mission fulfilled

Just as this *Year Book* records new communities, it also wishes to acknowledge the contribution of some whose work has now been completed. The last surviving members of several communities have died since the text of the last *Year Book* was finalised.

Perhaps the most widely-known was **Mother Christine CSKE,** who died on 17 March 1998. She had celebrated sixty years in profession the previous Autumn. The Community of St Katherine of Egypt (or of Alexandria, as it was sometimes known) was founded in 1879 by Paulina Granville. She was much older than the usual age for a Mother Foundress - well on in her fifties - but she made up for this by living to be over a hundred and ruling the community until she was ninety. The sisters' main work was with orphans in London. Sadly, in 1944, their Fulham convent was destroyed in a bombing raid and, after some years of having no home, the community settled in 1947 at Parmoor House near Henley on Thames (formerly the residence of exiled King Zog of Albania). Here the sisters looked after elderly women. The community was always small in numbers and Mother Christine, active almost to the end in serving others, was the last surviving sister. She was buried in the grounds of the Convent, which is now a Sue Ryder home.

Sister Margaret Mary SSM, who died on 12 June 1998 at the age of 91, was the last sister of the Society of the Servants of Mary. Founded in 1919, they were a 'daughter' community of CSMV, Wantage, and it was there that the community began. They moved to Camberwell, in London, in 1943, where they cared for the elderly and infirm. In later years, as their numbers declined, they moved to Abingdon, and then eventually the last sisters returned to Wantage.

Sister May CP, the last member of the Community of the Presentation died on 9 January 1999, aged 85, in the 47th year of her profession. Her community was originally called the Nursing Community of Christ the Consoler and was founded in 1927 to revive the vocational sense of nursing. Although its membership never grew to more than eleven sisters, the community ministered to many at its nursing home in Highgate and at St Saviour's Hospital, Osnaburgh Street. (The latter had been originally built between 1850 and 1852 as a convent for the Park Village Sisterhood, the first Anglican sisterhood established in the revival of Religious Life in the Church of England.) As the sisters grew older, they left London for Hythe in Kent, where eventually several CSF sisters went to support them in their community life. Sister May was the last survivor and in 1997 moved with CSF to Birmingham, where she died.

News from OHP

The year 1998 was an eventful one in the life of OHP, with a new Prioress (Sister Judith) installed in May; the celebration of two Golden Jubilees (Sisters Ursula and Barbara Maude); one Life Profession (Sister Pam); the Clothing of two novices (Sisters Graça and Adèle); and coming up in November 1999 is the Diamond Jubilee of Sister Bridget Mary, who is the last remaining sister from the little band that went to Canada in 1940 when St Hilda's School was hastily evacuated.

The educational development work in Swaziland has recently taken a step forward with the opening of another Skills Centre at Siteki, in the eastern region. Sister Judith's long involvement in this field, as also in the Duke of Edinburgh Award Scheme, contributed to her receiving the OBE in the 1999 New Year's Honours list.

At the Mother House, the major development is in the conversion of the premises of the former St Hilda's School, closed in July 1997, into the Sneaton Castle Centre. Although this venture had its official opening only in September 1998, it has already begun to establish itself as an attractive venue for visiting groups from near and far. Bookings for the coming year include several for Religious: the Leaders' and Novice Guardians' conferences, and the biennial gathering of monastic guest-masters/mistresses venturing north for the first time. An initiative for the year 2000 may bring boatloads of young people to Whitby on the 'Celtic M25', the sea-routes frequented by monks of an earlier age.

Trevor Huddleston CR (1913-1998)

Archbishop Trevor Huddleston CR died at Mirfield on 20 April 1998 aged 84. He will be chiefly remembered by many for his prophetic witness against the evils of the racist apartheid system in South Africa. This came first whilst he was resident in South Africa from 1943-56, during which years apartheid was being imposed and against which he vigorously campaigned. Then in later years, he was prominent in the Anti-Apartheid Movement, of which he was a founder in 1959 and later its President. A friend of Oliver Tambo and Nelson Mandela, it was moving and fitting that he lived to attend the latter's inauguration as President of South Africa in 1994, following the eventual establishment of a multi-racial political system, after so many years of struggle.

His work for the Church in a wider context was varied and challenging. He was Bishop of Masasi, in Tanzania, in the 1960s, followed by ten years in Stepney (London), before becoming Bishop of Mauritius and Archbishop of the Indian Ocean (1978-83).

Father Trevor Huddleston CR with President Mandela of South Africa

But undergirding it all was his vocation as a Religious. After being ordained in 1936 to a curacy in Swindon, he entered the Community of the Resurrection in 1939, and took vows in 1941. The community then sent him to South Africa and it was obedience to the community that brought him back in 1956, when he was recalled to be Novice Master. In his successive ministries for the Church, he took the disciplines and charism of Religious Life with him. After all his travels and responsibilities, it was to the community house at Mirfield that he finally retired and it was there that he died. Father Crispin Harrison CR, Superior of the Community of the Resurrection reflected that the Community of the Resurrection had, "lost a prayerful and diligent priest, and campaigner for the Gospel."

CHN in Peterborough, UK

In 1998, some CHN sisters went to live among the people of a housing estate at Welland, near Peterborough, after the local priest, the Vicar of Dogsthorpe, asked if CHN could provide a 'Christian presence' there. It is a deprived area economically, which feels cut off from the rest of the parish by three playing fields and two schools, and a major road which forms its boundary to the north. The church is in the more prosperous part of the parish and is very lively, but few people from Welland attend services there.

The Sisters live in a council house, the small bedroom of which is used as a chapel and in which the Eucharist is celebrated twice a week. The Vicar and other people join the Sisters in saying Morning and Evening Prayer there as well. There are good ecumenical contacts with the Methodists and Roman Catholics in the parish.

One of the sisters writes, "Like hundreds of council estates across the UK, there are many people living in Welland who are unemployed, many single parents with small children and quite a few lonely elderly people. All the problems so often reported in the newspapers can be encountered here: crime, drugs, etc. However, the great majority of people are trying against the odds to live life peacably and well. They are welcoming and kind to us. Sisters do some visiting and help one or two 'excluded' children."

Some of the chaplaincy team at the Lambeth Conference 1998, including the eight Anglican Religious (see opposite page).

News Round-up

Jubilee Rally *16 May 1998*

Anglican Religious have been supportive of the Jubilee 2000 campaign, which aims to have the unrepayable debts of many developing countries cancelled as a celebration of the Millennium. Some Religious were able to attend a large demonstration at Birmingham (UK) in May 1998, when many people linked hands in a long human chain around the venue of the G8 conference. This conference is a regular gathering of the leaders of the world's economically powerful countries.

Archbishop visits CSMV *21 May 1998*

The Archbishop of Canterbury visited Wantage for Ascension Day to celebrate with the sisters of the Community of St Mary the Virgin as they marked 150 years since their community was founded in 1848.

CSJD Anniversary Celebrations *11 July 1998*

Another 150th anniversary was marked in July by a special service in the cathedral in Birmingham in the UK. It was the anniversary of the founding of the Community of St John the Divine on 13 July 1848. It was originally established as a nursing order, although today the sisters have a variety of ministries. The large number of people who attended the service meant that the cathedral's galleries had to be opened to seat them all, and, after a joyous Mass, there was a delicious buffet lunch in the south aisle. The community's past was honoured in a moving and witty sermon by Bishop Hugh Montefiore: their future work encouraged and affirmed by the presence of so many friends and supporters.

Lambeth Conference *18 July - 9 August 1998*

Anglican Religious provided a chaplaincy team for the Lambeth Conference, the decennial meeting of the bishops of the Anglican Communion. For those on the team, it was a busy but rewarding few weeks. Their task was one of hospitality, supportive interaction and maintaining a round of prayer through the Daily Office and Bible study.

World Debt Debate *24 July 1998*

About eighty Anglican Religious attended the Lambeth Conference debate on world debt. The Archbishop of Canterbury acknowledged their presence at the beginning of the session, warmly expressing gratitude for the prayer and service Religious contribute to the Church's mission. The debate included a video, made by Christian Aid and an address by the Chair of the World Bank.

Meeting of Episcopal Visitors at Lambeth *3 August 1998*

Bishops who act as Visitors to Religious communities throughout the world were invited to meet during the Lambeth Conference, so that matters of mutual concern could be discussed. Despite other events in the hectic Lambeth schedule coinciding with this meeting, some fifty Bishops were able to attend. About twenty-five

Religious leaders also came to the meeting, and the session was chaired by Archbishop Michael Peers from Canada. The participants heard short talks by Dr Petà Dunstan, Abbot Basil OSB, Mother Jean Mary CHN and Bishop Richard Harries of Oxford, before a discussion was held on the rôle of the bishop in the life of a community.

UK Junior/First Professed Conference — *19-22 October 1998*

A conference of ten sisters in first profession, each from a different community, took place at Tymawr Convent in October 1998.

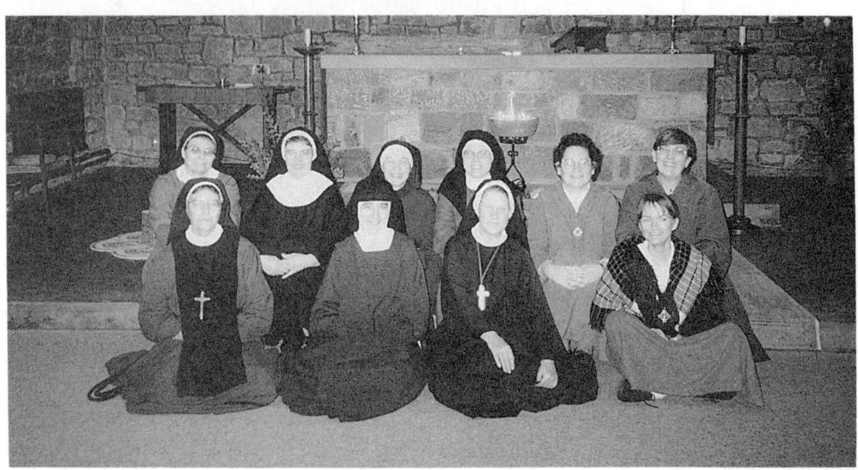

Led by Mother Mary Jean SSC and Sister Gillian Mary SSC, the participants had as the theme of their conference: From 'the community for myself' to 'myself for the community'. This is a quotation from Jean Vanier's book, *Community and Growth.* Vanier maintains that only when a majority of the members of a community make that transition can the group truly become a community. 'This is the movement from egoism to love, from death to resurrection; it is the Easter, the passover of the Lord. It is also the passing from a land of slavery to a promised land, the land of interior freedom.'

As Sister Joan SSC, one of the participants, reported, 'During our time together, we explored how we make this important transition through listening, discussion, sharing and pilgrimage. Everyone who took part greatly appreciated the opportunity of meeting together.'

The next conference is scheduled for Autumn 1999, again at Tymawr.

Contemplative Challenge 2000 — *21-25 June 1999*

Organised ecumenically by women's contemplative communities in the UK, a conference was held at St John's College of Ripon and York in June 1999. It had the title *Contemplative Challenge 2000: the Heart of the Matter* and was a celebration for the birth of Christ and for the gift of monastic and contemplative life in the Church.

About one hundred and sixty Religious, both men and women, attended, representing around sixty communities. The conference timetable was planned so that the participants could maintain their usual routine of personal and liturgical prayer. Each day began in York Minster with a period of silent prayer and the Office of Lauds. The talks - the main speaker was Father Bernardo Olivera OCSO, the Father General of the Cistercian Order - plenary sessions and other Offices were all at the College. The special Service of Celebration on the Thursday afternoon in the Minster, by kind permission of the Dean and Chapter, was an open occasion to which members of the general public were welcome. The preacher was the Rt Revd Jack Nicholls, Bishop of Sheffield. Over five hundred people attended.

Golden Jubilee of Clares *23-24 January 2000*

In January 2000, the Community of St Clare celebrates fifty years of life at St Mary's Convent at Freeland in Oxfordshire. The tentative beginnings of the community had come in the 1940s, when two aspirants began a common life in rooms in Wantage under the guidance of a CSMV sister. After a time based in Cassington, the Clares moved to Tymawr Convent in Monmouthshire in 1947, the home of the Society of the Sacred Cross. Although the Clares remained distinct from the host community, Mother Gvenrede SSC helped them to form their Rule and develop their life, until in January 1950 they moved to their own home at Freeland. This date therefore marks their formal foundation as an independent community.

Conference 2000 *4-7 September 2000*

A special conference of Anglican Religious is to be held in September 2000 to mark the second Millennium since the birth of Jesus. It is hoped that there will be a large gathering at Swanwick with participants drawn from many different communities. The Archbishop of Canterbury expects to visit the Conference, and the main speakers will be Bishop Rowan Williams and Mother Rosemary SLG. In the afternoons, workshops are planned: themes include dance, clowning, music, history, storytelling, and it is hoped that Professor John Polkinghorne will lead a session on the dialogue between science and religion.

Forthcoming Anniversaries

The All Saints Sisters will celebrate 150 years of the beginnings of their community in 2001. The 18 October 1851 was the date on which Mother Harriet Byron, their foundress, took up residence in Mortimer Street in London to live the Religious Life. Either side of the ASSP anniversary are two 150th anniversaries for the Community of St John Baptist, resident at Clewer in the UK and Mendham, NJ, in the USA. The foundress of CSJB, Mother Harriet Monsell, was clothed as a Sister on Ascension Day 1851 and professed on 30 November 1852.

Both ASSP and CSJB grew very quickly in the decades that followed their foundations and Sisters of both communities have worked in locations throughout the Anglican communion. They have achieved much in nursing, teaching and social work in their century and a half of service and prayer. So there is much to celebrate, and for which to give thanks, in these various anniversaries.

Website

The *Anglican Religious Communities Year Book* now has a Website. It can be found at: **http://www.orders.anglican.org/arcyb/**

Book Choice

Susan Mumm, STOLEN DAUGHTERS, VIRGIN MOTHERS: Anglican Sisterhoods in Victorian Britain.

Leicester UP, London, 1998, £45, hardback ISBN: 0-7185-0151-9

This is a significant book. Years of research into the nineteenth-century records of Anglican women's communities have given Susan Mumm an authoritative voice in tracing their formation and development. The study looks at how the communities were run and structured, the kind of women who were drawn to them, the work they performed. But it also looks at reactions to the sisterhoods, among clergy and among the general public. So the book reveals the community identities both from within and without the convent boundaries.

It is an academic book, with footnotes and statistics to back up the shrewd and thoughtful analysis; yet it reads well and is accessible to a more general audience. It is essential reading for anyone wishing to understand the complicated - and often stormy - history of the revival of women's communities in the Church of England.

Isobel Losada, NEW HABITS: Today's Women who choose to become Nuns.

Hodder & Stoughton, London, 1999, £12.99, paperback ISBN: 0-340-72238-X

Readers of the first edition of *ARCYB* will remember an interview with Teresa Mary SSB in which she shared some of the story of her call to Religious Life. Now the full interview, along with nine others conducted by Isobel Losada, has been published in book form. Reading these personal stories, shared with honesty and vulnerability, one is struck by both the integrity of the sisters concerned and the universality of the call to Religious Life. The diversity of these sisters' backgrounds is witness to the power of the Religious vocation even in a secular and agnostic environment.

The tabloid publicity at the book's launch concentrated on the comments about relationships and celibacy. However, the strength and vision of the book is in the theology of the call which the sisters articulate. All of them share candidly their thoughts and experiences of the power of God in their lives. Here are moving and powerful testimonies to the overcoming of pain and suffering and disadvantage, as well as the joys of gifts generously bestowed. It is an inspiring read.

Gillian Wilson (editor), THEODORE: Letters from the Oxford Mission in India 1946-1993.

Oxford Mission, Romsey, 1997, £12.95, paperback ISBN: 0-9532288-0-0

Available from Thameslink, 4 York Avenue, Windsor, Berkshire, SL4 3PD

The editor has assembled extracts from the letters of Father Theodore Mathieson BE (1946-94). They provide a vivid narrative of life in India during the last half century, and an insight into the work of an Anglican community in the developing world. Father Theodore was very concerned with training for employment, and founded both an industrial school and a self-employment centre. He also used his own talents as a musician to teach music to generations of students. The book is well-illustrated with photographs in colour as well as black and white.

This is a warm and affectionate book and deserves a wide readership.

Organisations

AFRICA

Council for the Religious Life

(in Southern Africa)

All Religious communities in the Church of the Province of Southern Africa come under the Council for the Religious Life. This is chaired by the Archbishop of Cape Town or a diocesan bishop nominated by him. There are eight members: two nominated by Episcopal Synod, three Religious nominated by the Council and three Religious nominated by the heads of the communities. All have four-year terms of office.

Council Members:

Rt Revd Edward Mackenzie (*Episcopal appointee*)
Sister Lucia CHN (Lesotho)
Sister Ntombi CHN (KwaZulu/Natal)
Sister Margaret Magdalen CSMV
Father Kingston Erson CR (*Secretary*)
Father Ralph Martin SSM
Sister Maureen OHP (*co-opted Treasurer*)

AUSTRALIA & NEW ZEALAND

Advisory Council for Religious Communities in Australasia

The Council consists of all the leaders of the Religious Communities in Australia and New Zealand, plus two bishops and two priests appointed by the Primate of Australia.

Bishops on the Council:	Rt Revd David McCall, Bishop of Willochra
	Rt Revd David Murray, Assistant Bishop of Perth
Priests on the Council:	Revd John Steward
	Revd Julia Perry
Secretary of the Council:	Father Christopher Myers SSM
	14 St John Street, Adelaide, SA 5000, AUSTRALIA

EUROPE

Advisory Council on the Relations of Bishops & Religious Communities

(commonly called 'The Advisory Council')

Rt Revd David Smith, Bishop of Bradford *(Chair)*
Most Revd & Rt Hon David Hope, Archbishop of York
Rt Revd Richard Harries, Bishop of Oxford
Rt Revd Jack Nicholls, Bishop of Sheffield

Communities' elected representatives (next election due 2000):

Sister Alison OHP
Abbot Basil Matthews OSB
Father Christopher Lowe CR
Brother Damian SSF
Father Gregory CSWG
Mother Jean Mary CHN
Sister Lillian CSA
Sister Margaret Angela CSJD
Sister Pamela CAH
Sister Tessa SLG

Co-opted member: Revd Sister Elizabeth Mary CSD
Roman Catholic Observer: Father Fergus Kelly CM

Pastoral Secretary: Revd David Platt *Tel: 01235 814729*
Administrative Secretary: Miss Jane Melrose,
Church House, Great Smith Street, London SW1P 3NZ
Tel: 0207 898 1379 *E-Mail: jane.melrose@c-of-e.org.uk*

Conference of the Leaders of Anglican Religious Communities (CLARC)

The Conference meets in full once a year, usually in June.

Steering Committee 1999-2000

Sister Anita CSC (2002)
Mother Ann Verena CJGS (2002) (*Secretary*)
Mother Barbara Claire CSMV (2001)
Mother Christine CSJD (2000)
Father Crispin CR (2001)
Father Douglas SSM (2002)
Sister Joyce CSF (2000)
Sister Judith OHP (2001)
Mother Sheila CAH (2001)

(dates indicate the year that the member's elected term ends)

The General Synod of the Church of England

Representatives of Lay Religious, Province of Canterbury

Sister Hilary CSMV **Elected 1995**

Chapter House, 20 Dean's Yard, London SW1P 3PA
Tel: 0207 222 5152 *Fax: 0207 233 2072*

Brother Tristam SSF **Elected 1994; Re-elected 1995**

The Friary of St Francis, Hilfield, Dorchester, Dorset DT2 7BE
Tel: 01300 341160 *Fax: 01300 341293*
E-Mail: Tristam@ssf.orders.anglican.org

Representative of Ordained Religious, Province of Canterbury

Revd Sister Teresa CSA **Elected 1995**

St Andrew's House, 2 Tavistock Road, Westbourne Park,
London W11 1BA
Tel: 0207 229 2662 *Fax: 0207 792 5993*
E-Mail: sister.teresa@dlondon.org.uk

Representative of Lay Religious, Province of York

Sister Margaret Shirley OHP **Elected 1990; Re-elected 1995**

St Oswald's Pastoral Centre, Woodlands Drive, Sleights,
Whitby YO21 1RY *Tel: 01947 810496*

Representative of Ordained Religious, Province of York

Father Aidan Mayoss CR **Elected 1993; Re-elected 1995**

House of the Resurrection, Mirfield, West Yorkshire WF14 0BN
Tel: 01924 494318 *Fax: 01924 492738*
E-Mail: amayoss@mirfield.org.uk

Communities Consultative Council (CCC)

The Communities Consultative Council was set up in 1975 and consists of elected representatives from Anglican Religious Communities in England. The Council has an annual conference each September. During 1998-99, proposals have been discussed for creating a new body - **Anglican Religious Communities (ARC)** - and these changes may take place in the Autumn of 1999. The item in the News section (page 2) gives more information.

All enquiries should be addressed to: Anglican Religious Communities, Church House, Great Smith Street, Westminster, London SW1P 3NZ.

North America

Conference on the Religious Life in the Anglican Communion in the Americas (CORL)

The purpose of CORL is to provide opportunities for mutual support and sharing among its member communities and co-ordinate their common interests and activities, to engage in dialogue with other groups, to present a coherent understanding of the Religious Life to the Church and to speak as an advocate for the Religious Orders to the Church. CORL is incorporated as a non-profit organization in both Canada and the USA.

Brother Justus Van Houten SSF (*President*)
Sister Pamela Clare CSF (*Vice-President*)
Sister Constance Joanna Gefvert SSJD (*Secretary-Treasurer*)

The Revd Dr Donald Anderson (*General Secretary*)
31 Island View Drive, RR#1, Little Britain, Ontario K0M 2C0, CANADA.
Tel & Fax: 705 786 3330 *E-Mail: da@ecunet.org*

Publications (contact the General Secretary)
1: Directory of the Members of the Conference on the Religious Life in the Americas 1997
2: Handbook of Guidelines for Anglican Religious Communities, Solitary Religious, and those taking private Religious Vows, in Canada and the United States, 1992

House of Bishops Standing Committee on Religious Communities in the Anglican Church of Canada

The Committee usually meets twice a year, during the House of Bishops meeting. Its rôle is consultative and supportive.

Most Revd Michael Peers, Archbishop & Primate of Canada
Most Revd Arthur Peters, Archbishop of Nova Scotia & Metropolitan of the Ecc. Province of Canada (*Chair*)
Rt Revd Barry Jenks, Bishop of British Columbia
Rt Revd Bruce Stavert, Bishop of Quebec
The Superiors of CSC, OHC, SSJD & SSJE
Revd Dr Donald Anderson, General Secretary of CORL
Revd Gordon Light, Principal Secretary to the Primate (*Secretary*)

Synod of the Anglican Church of Canada

Religious Synod members:
Sister Constance Joanna SSJD
Sister Michael CSC

ECUMENICAL & INTER-DENOMINATIONAL

Conference of Religious (CoR)

The Conference of Religious is open to all Roman Catholic Provincial leaders of Religious Congregations in England and Wales. The leaders of Anglican communities may be Associate members, which, apart from voting rights, means they receive all the same benefits and information as the Roman Catholic leaders.

CoR is run by an executive committee, elected from its members, which meets every two months. It deals with matters affecting men and women Religious, and various matters of interest to them. There is particular emphasis on peace and justice issues. Members of the executive also plan the day General Meeting in September and the residential Annual General Meeting and Conference held in Swanwick, Derbyshire, in January as well as representing the members on various associations and bodies. The secretarial staff deal with the administration and produce a monthly mailing full of useful information.

General Secretary of CoR:
Sister Lorna Brockett RSCJ, CoR Secretariat, 114 Mount Street, London W1Y 6AH
Tel: 0207 493 1817 Fax: 0207 409 2321 E-Mail: confrelig@aol.com

The Anglican representative on the CoR Executive Committee:
Sister Joyce CSF, 43 Endymion Road, Brixton, London SW2 2BU
Tel & Fax: 0208 674 5344 E-Mail: Joycecsf@aol.com

Care & Housing of Elderly Religious Project (CHERP)

The aims of CHERP are to enable Religious to make the best possible provision for the care of their elderly, sick and infirm members. This is done by the operation of a helpline, the organisation of conferences on matters of common concern, encouraging joint ventures between communities and other organisations, liaison with administrators and health authorities, and co-operation with nursing and hospital management bodies. The project was set up under the aegis of CoR, ABC and CLARC. It publishes a Newsletter three times a year (March, July and November) in order to disseminate information.

Project Co-ordinator:
Ellen Thomas
Fieldworker:
Janet Norman
CHERP Office
3 Bute Gardens
London W6 7DR
Tel: 0208 846 9681; Fax: 0208 748 4058

Anglican Representative:
Mother Frances Anne CSD
19 The Close,
Salisbury,
Wiltshire SP1 2EE
Tel: 01722 339761

Association of British Contemplatives (ABC)

The Association of British Contemplatives (ABC) is constituted by the women's contemplative communities of England, Scotland and Wales, Roman Catholic and Anglican. The purpose of the Association is: To foster solidarity and mutual co-operation between all the women's contemplative communities. To co-ordinate, if and when desired, initiatives and projects of mutual concern. To strengthen contemplative vision and values in the Church. To provide a structure for responding to current issues of concern To provide a channel of communication with the various Hierarchies and other official bodies.

The ABC Executive:

Abbess Joanna Jamieson OSB *(Chair)*, Stanbrook Abbey, Worcester WR2 4TD
Mother Mary of St Michael ODC *(Deputy Chair)*
Mother Rosemary SLG *(Anglican Representative)*
Mother Aelred Casey OSC
Sister Christina SA *(Treasurer)*

Kaire

Kaire aims to be 'a living interconfessional cell' of persons engaged in monastic, diaconal or active call in their Church and in the world. Its ecumenical charism, moved by the Spirit, is to a conversion to prayer, to one another, and to Unity.

Kaire emerged from a 1971 ecumenical meeting of sisters and deaconesses, organised by DIAKONIA (World Federation of Sisterhoods and Diaconal Associations), with Anglican, Orthodox, Protestant and Roman Catholic participants. In order to continue the thinking and experience of that first meeting, Kaire was created and since then has held meetings every year or two, attended by sometimes twenty, sometimes as many as seventy people, in locations all over Europe. Care is given to the balance of confessions, countries and forms of ministry.

The next meeting in Autumn 2000 will probably take place in Hungary. For further information contact: Sister Marie Paul Six, Kaire Secrétariat, 15b rue Porte d'Allemagne, F-57930 Fenetrange, FRANCE. *Tel: 87 07 50 25* *Fax: 87 07 54 33*

Permanent International Ecumenical Consultation (PIEC)

In 1977, through the initiative of Father Pedro Arrupe SJ and Brother Michael SSF, an ecumenical consultation of male Religious superiors was held to encourage contact and the exchange of ideas. After the second consultation in 1979, the gathering developed into a yearly meeting, including both men and women, from among the Anglican, Lutheran, Orthodox, Reformed and Roman Catholic traditions. The consultation is informal and takes place in different locations.

The current Anglican representatives are Mother Rosemary SLG from Fairacres in Oxford and Father Crispin Harrison CR from Mirfield.

Gladstone's Library
St Deiniol's

Hawarden Flintshire CH5 3DF Wales

Tel. 01244 532350 Fax. 01244 520643
E-mail deiniol.visitors@btinternet.com

Britain's Finest Residential Library

LIBRARY

- 200,000 books, periodicals and pamphlets in Arts and Humanities.
- We specialise in Theology and History, but there are also good collections of Literature, Philosophy and Classics.
- The Bishop Moorman Franciscan Collection is Britain's largest private collection of material on St Francis and the early Franciscans.

ACCOMMODATION

- Comfortable bedrooms and excellent food in delightful surroundings.

SABBATICALS

- An ideal environment for a sabbatical. Visiting scholars are welcome to use the facilities of University College Chester.

PROGRAMME

- A programme of courses, seminars, day-conferences is arranged each year on a variety of Theological and Victorian Studies themes with leading scholars.

CHAPEL

- Morning Prayer, Evening Prayer and Eucharist are held in the Chapel.

CLERGY AND RELIGIOUS DISCOUNT

- Special low rates are offered to clergy and religious wanting to make use of the Library.

CONFERENCE / GROUP BOOKINGS

- Conference facilities are available for residential or day groups.

HOLIDAY

- A relaxed place to study but also near to some of Britain's most breathtaking countryside and ancient monuments. - Snowdonia, the Roman City of Chester, and the castles and beautiful gardens of Wales.

Please write to the Bookings Secretary at the above address for details
or email via our Webpage:

www.btinternet.com/~st.deiniols/homepage.htm

Directory of Communities

This Directory contains entries for Religious communities from throughout the Anglican Communion. Most have listed their members (either in profession order or alphabetically) and have provided information, where appropriate, on their guest accommodation, publications and the services and crafts they have for sale.

There are an estimated 2,600 Religious in the Anglican Communion, (*1,000 men and 1,600 women*).

The approximate regional totals are:

Africa:	420	(*Men 50, Women 370*)
Asia:	80	(*Men 20, Women 60*)
Australasia & Pacific:	800	(*Men 575, Women 225*)
Europe:	940	(*Men 230, Women 710*)
North America & Caribbean:	360	(*Men 100, Women 260*)

INTERNATIONAL TELEPHONING

Telephone numbers in this directory are listed as used within the country concerned. To use them internationally, first dial the international code followed by the country code (see list below).

Country	Code	Country	Code
Australia	+ 61	Korea	+ 82
Bangladesh	+ 880	Lesotho	+ 266
Canada	+ 1	New Zealand	+ 64
Fiji	+ 679	PNG	+ 675
France	+ 33	Solomon Islands	+ 677
Ghana	+ 233	South Africa	+ 27
Haiti	+ 509	Swaziland	+ 268
India	+ 91	Tanzania	+ 255
Republic of Ireland	+ 353	UK	+ 44
Japan	+ 81	USA	+ 1

Society of All Saints Sisters of the Poor

ASSP

Founded 1851

All Saints Convent
St Mary's Road
Oxford
OX4 1RU
UK

Tel: 01865 249127
Fax: 01865 726547

Mattins
6.30 am

Eucharist or Terce
9.00 am

Midday Office or Eucharist
12.00 noon

Vespers
5.30 pm

Compline
8.00 pm

Office book:
ASSP Office

Registered Charity:
No. 228383

As All Saints Sisters of the Poor, we believe we are called to be alongside the homeless and unemployed, the sick, the dying, the bereaved, the old, the lonely - any who welcome the friendship we offer as companions journeying together. In Oxford the community has pioneered: St John's Home, a residential home for elderly people; Helen House, a hospice offering respite and terminal care for children with life-limiting illness and support for their families; the Porch, a drop-in refreshment centre for the homeless and unemployed; and a church embroidery centre. In the London house, there are also many opportunities for ministry and mission. Pastoral visiting, preaching and public speaking, hospitality and spiritual direction are some of the ways in which we live out our calling.

Undergirding all this activity is the daily round of celebrating the liturgy together, with opportunity and commitment to set aside time for prayer, reading, and waiting upon God. We set aside time for one another, respecting cherishing and caring for one another over the years. It is only in being with God and with one another, amidst all the activity, that we come to know the true purpose and calling of our lives.

SISTER HELEN ASSP
(Mother Superior, assumed office 29 September 1989)
SISTER FRANCES DOMINICA ASSP *(Assistant Superior)*

Sister Alice
Sister Marian
Sister Elisabeth May
Sister Barbara Mary
Sister Margaret
Sister Jean Margaret
Sister Elizabeth Mary
Sister Helen Mary
Sister Mary Julian
Sister Ann Frances
Sister Margaret Anne

Obituaries

29 Oct 1998 — Sister Dorothy Hilda, aged 91, professed 61 years
3 Mar 1999 — Sister Pauline, aged 101, member of the community for 46 years

Community Publication

New Venture, published annually in December. Order from the Society of All Saints.

Community Wares

The Embroidery Centre makes, repairs and remounts vestments, frontals etc.

Community History
Peter Mayhew, *All Saints: Birth & Growth of a Community*, ASSP, Oxford, 1987.

Other Addresses
St John's Home
(for the elderly)
St Mary's Road
Oxford OX4 1QE
UK
Tel: 01865 247725
Fax: 01865 247920

Helen House
(children's hospice)
37 Leopold Street
Oxford OX4 1QT
UK
Tel: 01865 728251
Fax: 01865 749829

The Church
Embroidery Centre
All Saints Convent
St Mary's Road
Oxford OX4 1RU
UK
Tel: 01865 248627

The Porch
All Saints Convent
St Mary's Road
Oxford OX4 1RU
UK
Tel: 01865 728545

All Saints House
82 Margaret Street
London W1N 8LH
UK
Tel: 0207 637 7818
Fax: 0207 636 5364

The Chapel, All Saints Convent, Oxford

Guest and Retreat Facilities
There is a small guest house with four rooms, and also a small flatlet, at All Saints' Convent in Oxford. Private retreats are possible by arrangement.

Associates
Those in sympathy with the aims of the community are invited to become Associates or Priest Friends.

Brotherhood of the Ascended Christ

BAC

Founded 1877

Brotherhood House
7 Court Lane
Delhi 110054
INDIA
Tel: 11 396 8515
or 11 293 1432
Fax: 11 398 1025
E-Mail:
mono@del2.vsnl.net.in

Morning Worship & Eucharist
6.05 am

Forenoon Prayer (Terce)
8.00 am

Midday Prayer (Sext)
12.45 pm

Afternoon Prayer (None)
3.50 pm

Evening Worship
7.30 pm

Night Prayer (Compline)
9.10 pm

Office Book:
The Church of North India Book of Worship
&
The Lesser Hours & Night Prayer (BAC)

Today, the Brotherhood has five presbyters and one deacon who belong to the Church of North India. Since the earliest days, the Brotherhood has had a concern for serving the poor and underprivileged. In 1975, the Delhi Brotherhood Society was set up to organise social development projects in the poorer parts of Delhi. The work and social outreach of the Brotherhood is with and not for the poor of Delhi. The Brotherhood has initiated programmes of community health, education, vocational training and programmes for street and working children.

COLLIN THEODORE BAC
(*Head, elected 24 November 1997*)
IAN WEATHRALL BAC (*Deputy Head*)
James Stuart
Amos Rajamoney
Monodeep Daniel
Solomon George
Postulants: 2

Other address
Ashanekitan, DBS Centre, Shahidnagar, Dist. Ghaziabad, Uttar Pradesh, INDIA.
(Postal address is c/o The Brotherhood House in Delhi.)

Guest and Retreat Facilities
The Brotherhood House at Court Lane has a large garden and well-stocked library. It is used as a centre for retreats, quiet days and conferences. The small Guest Wing receives visitors from all over the world.

The Brotherhood House, Delhi

Brotherhood of the Epiphany

BE

Founded 1879

Oxford Mission
Bogra Road
PO Box 21
Barisal 8200
BANGLADESH

TEL: 0431 53866
& 54481

Mattins

Prime

Eucharist

Terce

Sext

None

Evensong

Compline

Office Book:
Church of Bangladesh Book of Common Prayer
&
Oxford Mission Office Book
(modified 1993)

The Community was founded in 1879 in response to an appeal to the University of Oxford by the Bishop of Calcutta, India, for work to be done among the educated people of the city. The brothers lived and worked close to the University.

Later, branch houses were formed at Behala, Barisal and Jobarpar. The partition of India in 1947 resulted in the separation of the work in India and the work in what is now Bangladesh.

With the death of the Fathers in India, the work there is carried on by a priest of the Church of North India. The work of the Mission continues at Barisal under the supervision of the Church of Bangladesh where the Mission runs boarding schools, a Christian students' hostel, St Anne's Medical Centre, an orphanage and a primary school. The Brotherhood of the Epiphany and the Christa Seva Sangha (see separate entry) are both involved in this work.

FATHER FRANCIS PANDEY BE
(Father Superior, assumed office 1993)
Novices: 2
Brother Martin Mondol
Brother John Provudan Hira
Postulants: 2
Brother Benedict Biplob Baroi
Brother Newton Chakravarty

Address in India
Oxford Mission, Barisha, Calcutta 700 008, INDIA
Administrator: Father James Stevens

Community Publication
The Oxford Mission News, twice a year. Write to: Oxford Mission, PO Box 86, Romsey, Hampshire SO51 8YD
Tel: 01794 515004
Annual subscription costs £4.00, post free.

Community History
Brethren of the Epiphany, *A Hundred Years in Bengal,* ISPCK, Delhi, 1979.

Fellowship of the Epiphany
The Oxford Mission Fellowship of the Epiphany was founded in 1921 for friends of the Mission in India, Bangladesh, the British Isles and elsewhere.
Current membership:
India: 42; Bangladesh: 25; British Isles: 39; elsewhere: 3.

Chama cha Maria Mtakatifu

(Community of St Mary of Nazareth and Calvary)

CMM

Founded 1946

The Convent
Kilimani
SLP 502
Masasi
TANZANIA

Tel: 59 510126

Morning Prayer
5.30 am

Mass
6.30 am (7.00 am Sun)

Midday Prayer
12.30 pm

Evening Prayer
3.00 pm

Compline
8.30 pm

Office Book:
Zanzibar Prayer Book (Swahili)
&
The Daily Office SSF

The Community was founded by the former Bishop of Masasi, Rt Revd William Vincent Lucas, in 1946 and was brought up by the Sisters of the Community of the Sacred Passion. Our aim is to serve God by beoming closer to God's will under vows, and serving God's people and bringing them to know and love God, especially women and children. We are an international community and accept from any country girls and women who are willing to serve God.

The Sisters give help in looking after churches in parishes and teach Religious Education in primary schools and in Sunday schools. We have kindergarten schools and run development groups for girls. Some Sisters do nursing in hospitals and serve the needy, visit the sick and prisoners.

MOTHER SOPHIA CMM
(Revd Mother Superior, installed 21 August 1999)

SISTER JESSIE CMM (*Sister Superior, Ndola, Zambia*)
SISTER CECILIA CMM (*Sister Superior, Northern Zone*)

Sister May Elizabeth
Sister Magdalene
Sister Rehema
Sister Ethel Mary
Sister Neema
Sister Helena
Sister Ester
Sister Christina
Sister Martha Brijita
Sister Grace
Sister Tabitha
Sister Eunice Mary
Sister Joy
Sister Franciska
Sister Anjela
Sister Gloria
Sister Anna
Sister Priska
Sister Nesta
Sister Bertha
Sister Aneth
Sister Mary
Sister Agatha
Sister Valentina
Sister Lucy
Sister Berita
Sister Mercy Neema
Sister Lidia
Sister Stella
Sister Agnes Margareth
Sister Marina Felistas
Sister Jane
Sister Rabeka
Sister Dorothy
Sister Perpetua
Sister Jeniper
Sister Anjelina
Sister Julia Rehema
Sister Joceline Florence
Sister Jane Rose
Sister Susana Skolastica
Sister Upendo Perpetua
Sister Anna Beatrice
Sister Mariam Upendo
Sister Josephine Joyce
Sister Rose Joyce
Sister Skolastica Mercy
Sister Mary Priska
Sister Paulina Anna
Sister Janet Margaret
Sister Thekla Elizabeth
Sister Clauda Violet
Sister Janet Elizabeth

Sister Gloria Anjela	Sister Clara Skolastika	Sister Josephine Priska
Sister Edna Joana	Sister Jane Felistas	Sister Anna Mariam
Sister Lilian Martha	Sister Asnath Isabela	Sister Marcelina
Sister Josephine Brijita	Sister Brijita Elizabeth	
Sister Daines Charity	Sister Ethy Nyambeku	*Novices:* 22
Sister Agnes Edna	Sister Vumilia Imelda	*Postulants:* 10

Obituaries

6 Jun 1997	Sister Maria, aged 61, professed 41 years
7 Dec 1997	Sister Helena Mary, aged 28, professed 6 years
7 May 1998	Sister Fidea, aged 68, professed 49 years

Addresses of other houses

PO Box 116
Newala
Mtwara Region
TANZANIA

PO Box 162
Mtwara
TANZANIA

PO Box 45
Tanga
TANZANIA

PO Box 195
Korogwe
Tanga Region
TANZANIA

The Convent
PO Kwa Mkono Handeni
Tanga Region
TANZANIA

Ilala
PO Box 25016
Dar es Salaam
TANZANIA

PO Box 150
Njombe
TANZANIA

PO Box 6
Liuli
Mbinga-Ruvuma Region
TANZANIA

Sayuni Msima
PO Box 150
Njombe
TANZANIA

Ndola Convent
PO Box 70172
Ndola
ZAMBIA

Community Wares

Crafts, vestments, altar breads, agriculture products, cattle products.

Guest and Retreat Facilities

We have a guest house at the Mother House - Chanikanguo in Masasi. Visitors come and stay, some for a few days, others for weeks.

Chita Che Zita Rinoyera

(Holy Name Community)

CZR

Founded 1935

St Augustine's Mission
PO Penhalonga
Mutare
ZIMBABWE

Tel: Penhalonga 22217

Mattins or Morning Prayer

Mass

Midday Office

Evensong

Compline

Community Wares
We sell chickens, eggs, milk, cattle (two or three a year) and wafers.

Our Community was started in 1935 by Father Baker of the CR Fathers at Penhalonga, with Mother Isabella as the founder. The CZR Sisters were helped by CR Sisters (Liz and Lois), and later by OHP Sisters (especially Lila, Mary Francis, Joyce and Hannah). When they left, Sister Isabella was elected Mother.

Today the CZR Sisters work at the clinic and at the primary and secondary schools. Some do visiting and help teach the catechism. We make wafers for several dioceses, including Harare. Some of the Sisters look after the church, seeing to cleaning and mending of the church linen.

In 1982, half the Sisters and the novices left CZR and created another community at Bonda. Six months later, some of those Sisters in turn went to found Religious Life at Harare. In 1989, some of the Bonda community left to go to Gokwe and begin Religious Life there. So CZR has been the forerunner of three other communities in Zimbabwe.

Please pray that God may bless us.

MOTHER ISABELLA CZR
(*Revd Mother, assumed office 12 December 1996*)
SISTER MOTHER ANNA MARIA CZR (*Assistant Superior*)

Sister Stella Mary	Sister Betty
Sister Theresa	Sister Emelia
Sister Hilda Raphael	Sister Annamore
Sister Felicity	*Novices:* 1
Sister Elizabeth	*Postulants:* 3

Christa Sevika Sangha (Handmaids of Christ)

CSS

Founded 1970

Jobarpar
Barisal Division
Uz Agailjhara 8240
BANGLADESH

The Community was founded in 1970 and was under the care of the Sisterhood of the Epiphany until 1986, when its own Constitution was passed and Sister Susila SE was elected as Superior. The Sevikas supervise girls' hostels and a play-centre for small children. They also help in St Gabriel's School and supervise St Mary's Asroi (Home) at Barisal. The Community also produces for sale a wide variety of goods and produce (see below). The Visitor is the Bishop of the diocese.

MOTHER SUSILA CSS
(Mother Foundress, 25 January 1970;
elected Revd Mother CSS in July 1986)

Sister Ruth	Sister Margaret
Sister Jharna	Sister Kalyani
Sister Sobha	Sister Shefali
Sister Agnes	Sister Salome
Sister Dorothy	*Novices*: 3

Other Address
Oxford Mission, Bogra Road, PO Box 21, Barisal 8200, BANGLADESH
Tel: 0431 54481

Morning Prayer

Holy Communion

Midday Prayer

Quiet Prayer together

Evening Prayer

Compline

Community Wares
Vestments, children's clothes, embroidery work, wine, wafers, candles.
Farm produce: milk, poultry, fish.
Land produce: rice, fruit, coconuts & vegetables.
Ten books translated into Bengali are for sale.

Community Publication
The Oxford Mission News, twice a year. Write to Oxford Mission, PO Box 86, Romsey, Hampshire SO51 8YD
Tel: 01794 515004
Annual subscription costs £4.00, post free.

Office Book:
Church of Bangladesh Book of Common Prayer
&
Community Office Book
(all Offices are in Bengali)

Community History
Brethren of the Epiphany, *A Hundred Years in Bengal*, ISPCK, Delhi, 1979.

Fellowship of the Epiphany
The Oxford Mission Fellowship of the Epiphany was founded in 1921 for friends of the Mission in India, Bangladesh, the British Isles and elsewhere.
Current membership:
India: 42; Bangladesh: 25; British Isles: 39; elsewhere: 3.

Community of All Hallows

CAH

Founded 1855

All Hallows Convent
Belsey Bridge Road
Ditchingham
Bungay
Suffolk
NR35 2 DT
UK

Tel: 01986 892749
Fax: 01986 892731

Lauds
6.40 am
(7.30 am Sat & Sun)

Eucharist
7.15 am (9.30 am Sat, 10.00 am Sun)

Terce
9.30 am (weekdays only)

Sext
12 noon

None
2.00 pm

Evening Prayer
5.30 pm

Compline
8.45 pm

Office Book:
Daily Prayer; BCP & ASB Evensong on a regular basis.

A Registered Charity.

There is no typical All Hallows sister: we are as diverse in gifts and personality as are the Saints under whose patronage we try to live out the life to which God has called us. Central to the life of the Community is the daily Eucharist, the Divine Office and time for private prayer, meditation and spiritual reading.

The desire 'to serve Christ in one another and love as He loves us' overflows into the active life of the Community; into the welcome given to the many visitors to our three Guest Houses and our two Retreat and Conference Centres where Sisters are involved in the ministries of hospitality, spiritual direction and retreat giving.

The Community also cares for those with other needs – the very young at our day nursery and the elderly at our nursing/residential home. Our hospital is a special place for those needing to convalesce or having respite care, for day care, those needing physiotherapy and also for those nearing the end of their earthly pilgrimage. There is also a very loving concern and care for those who suffer from AIDS.

At the moment, there are no resident sisters in Norwich. This is by no means necessarily intended as permanent. The Community's commitment to the city remains foremost in our thoughts as we continue to explore God's way for us in our life and work there and elsewhere ... after all, our foundress herself came from Norwich!

All enquiries about the life and work of CAH should be directed in the first place to the Revd Mother CAH at the Convent.

MOTHER SHEILA CAH
(Revd Mother, assumed office 6 June 1995)
SISTER PAMELA CAH (*Assistant Superior*)

Sister Elizabeth
Mother Mary
Sister Florence
Sister Violet
Sister Daphne
Sister Jean
Sister Winifred
Sister Jean Margaret
Sister Margaret
Sister Winifred Mary
Sister Rebecca
Sister Edith Margaret
Sister Jane
Sister Louise
Sister Rhonda
Sister Mary
Sister Karen

Novices: 2

Obituaries

17 May 1998 Sister Matilda, aged 94, professed 49 years

Other addresses and telephone numbers

The following all share the same address as All Hallows Convent:

St Gabriel's Conference and Retreat House
Tel: 01986 892133 (staff) *01986 895765 (residents)*

Holy Cross Guest House
Tel: 01986 894092

All Hallows Guest House
Tel: 01986 892840

St Michael's Retreat Centre
Tel: 01986 895749 (staff)
01986 894607 (residents)

St Mary's Lodge
(House of silence & retreat)
Tel: 01986 892731

All Hallows Hospital
Station Road
Ditchingham
Bungay
Suffolk NR35 2QW
UK
Tel: 01986 892728

Adèle House
St John's Road
Bungay
Suffolk
NR35 1DL
UK
Tel: 01986 892643

Community Publication
A newsletter is circulated yearly at All Saints tide. To be included on the mailing list, please write to All Hallows Convent at the address above.

Community History
Sister Violet CAH, *All Hallows, Ditchingham*, Becket Publications, Oxford, 1983.
Mother Mary CAH, *Memories,* privately published 1998.
(A collection of memories and reflections primarily intended for friends and associates but available to all.)

Community Wares
A wide selection of photography cards, as well as some others.

Guest and Retreat Facilities
Enquiries about booking for the Retreat/Conference Centres should be addressed to the Convent Secretary at the Convent. Enquiries about staying at one of our guest houses should be addressed to the sister-in-charge of the relevant house.

Most convenient time to telephone: 7.00 pm - 8.30 pm (any day)
9.00 am - 12 noon, 2.15 pm - 4.30 pm (Monday to Friday)

Oblates and Associates
OBLATES, ASSOCIATES and CONTACT MEMBERS offer themselves to God within the community context in a varying degree of 'hands-on' commitment. Apply to the Convent for details.

Benedictine Community of Christ the King

CCK

Founded 1993

RMB 8601
Taminick Gap Road
South Wangaratta
Victoria 3678
AUSTRALIA
Tel: 3 5725 7343

Monastic Mattins & Prayer Time
4.30 am

Lauds
6.00 am

Eucharist & Terce
8.00 am

Sext
12 noon

None
3.00 pm

Vespers & Prayer Time
5.00 pm

Compline
7.45 pm

Office Book:
The Divine Office is based on the Sarum Rite, using APBA for the Psalms. Whenever the Office is sung, it is in Plainsong using BCP Psalms.

The Community of Christ the King is an Anglican Benedictine order, enclosed and contemplative. Its members endeavour to glorify God in a life of prayer under the threefold vow of Stability, Conversion of Life and Obedience. They follow a rhythm of life centred on the worship of God in the Daily Eucharist and sevenfold Office.

The convent nestles at the foot of the Warby Ranges, on a picturesque farm owned by the Diocese of Wangaratta. It is surrounded by attractive flower gardens, a citrus orchard and a kitchen garden. The fruit and vegetables ensure a certain amount of self-sufficiency, and affords the opportunity and privilege of manual labour, essential to the contemplative life.

Hospitality aimed at helping visitors deepen their spiritual lives through prayer is a feature of the life. The property with its extensive views, bush walks and seclusion is ideally suited to relaxation, quiet reflection and retreat. The property is ringed by fourteen large crosses providing opportunity for meditation on the way of the cross, and for prayer in solitude. We hold silent retreats and hope to develop this outreach.

MOTHER RITA MARY CCK
(*Revd Mother, assumed office 31 July 1997*)
SISTER PATIENCE CCK (*Assistant*)

Sister Clare
Sister Margery

Community Publication

The Community publishes a letter twice a year, sent free of charge to all interested in CCK (approximately 300 copies).

Guest and Retreat Facilities

We cater for those who want to deepen their life in Christ. There is a guest house which can accommodate three people (women or men). There is no charge. There is also a flat attached to the chapel and two caravans. A large fellowship room provides for parish quiet days and study groups.

Oblates

An Order of Benedictine Oblates has been established, open to women and men.

Community of the Companions of Jesus the Good Shepherd

CJGS

Founded 1920

*Convent of St John Baptist
Hatch Lane, Clewer
Windsor, Berkshire
SL4 3QR
UK*

Tel: 01753 850618

Lauds 7.30 am

Tierce 9.00 am (8.45 am Sun & major feasts)

Eucharist 9.10 am (9.00 am Sun & major feasts)

Midday Office 12.00 noon

Vespers 5.30 pm

Compline 8.45 pm (8.15 pm Sun)

Office Book: CSJB Office

Registered Charity No. 270317

When the Community was founded, the first Sisters were all teachers living alone or in small groups but coming together during the school holidays. In 1943, West Ogwell House in South Devon became the Mother House and the more usual form of conventual life was established as well. The work of Christian education has always been of primary concern to the Community, whether in England or overseas, although not all the Sisters have been teachers.

In 1996, the Community moved to Windsor to live and work alongside the Community of St John Baptist, while retaining its own ethos. The Community aims 'to express in service for others, Christ's loving care for his flock.' At present, this service includes involvement in lay and ordained local ministry training; offering companionship to those seeking to grow in the spiritual life through spiritual direction, quiet days and retreats; and especially the befriending of the elderly, lonely and those in need. Sisters are involved in Sunday school work and visiting a local day centre and residential homes.

MOTHER ANN VERENA CJGS
(Mother Superior, assumed office 20 March 1996)
SISTER ANGELA FELICITY *(Assistant Superior)*
Sister Evelyn Theresa
Sister Kathleen Frideswide

Obituaries

14 Oct 1998	Sister Phyllis Mary, aged 95, professed 46 years
17 Jan 1999	Sister Ena Florence, aged 90, professed 48 years

Community Publication
CJGS News. Contact the Mother Superior.

Community Wares
Calligraphy, candles.

Guest and Retreat Facilities
See under CSJB.

Associates
Associates of the Community are members of the Fellowship of St Augustine. They follow a rule of life drawn up with the help of one of the Sisters. They give support to the Community through their prayer, interest and alms, and are remembered in prayer by the Community. They and the Community say the 'Common Devotion' daily. They are truly our extended family.

Community of the Glorious Ascension

CGA

Founded 1960

Brothers:
The Priory
Start Point
Kingsbridge
Devon TQ7 2NG
UK

Tel & Fax:
01548 511474

Registered Charity:
No. 254524

The Community aims to combine a life of prayer and worship with that of going out to support itself through daily work. The brothers generally live in small groups bound together in the corporate pattern of monastic life. The mission of the Community is primarily that of being with and amongst people in ordinary situations.

BROTHER SIMON CGA
(Prior, assumed office 20 May 1993)

Community Publication
CGA Newsletter, published annually. Write to the Prior.

Guest and Retreat Facilities
The Priory in Devon is not simply a retreat facility, but aims to offer opportunity for relaxation, reflection or holiday by groups, individuals and families. The Community welcomes groups by day and has two rooms in the main house which comfortably accommodate ten people for gatherings and meetings. Self-catering accommodation is also available in cottages set in a converted barn adjacent to the main house. At times, it is possible to welcome guests to the main house for short stays in single and twin-bedded en-suite rooms, with meals taken with the Community.

Sisters:

Prasada
Quartier Subrane
83440 Montauroux
FRANCE

Tel & Fax:
04 94 47 74 26

Prasada is set on the edge of a Provençal hill village, where guests are welcome for a time of rest and refreshment. Many join the Community in their chapel for the Eucharist and Divine Office. The Sisters are also involved in various activities with the local English-speaking and French communities.

SISTER JEAN CGA (*Prioress*)
Revd Sister Cécile

Community of the Good Shepherd

CGS

Founded 1978

PO Box 17
90700 Sandakan
Sabah
East Malaysia

The CGS Sisters in Malaysia were formerly a part of the Community of the Companions of Jesus the Good Shepherd in the UK. They became an autonomous community in 1978. Their Rule is based on that of St Augustine and their ministry is mainly parish work.

Sister Oi Chin CGS
Sister Margaret Lin-Din CGS

Sisters Margaret Lin-Din and Oi Chin

Mother Ann Verena CJGS and Sister Margaret Lin-Din CGS with CGS associates in St Michael's Church, Sandekan

Benedictine Community of the Holy Cross, Rempstone

CHC

Founded 1857

Holy Cross Convent
Rempstone Hall
near Loughborough
LE12 6RG
UK
Tel: 01509 880336
Fax: 01509 881812

(Southwell Diocese)

Matins
6.55 am

Lauds
7.30 am

Terce
9.00 am

Sext 11.45 am
(12.10 Sun & Tue)

None
1.30 pm

Vespers 4.30 pm
(4.00 pm Thu)

Compline
8.00 pm

Mass
12.00 noon (9.30 am Sun, 9.15 am Tue)

The Community of the Holy Cross was founded in 1857 by Elizabeth Neale (sister of John Mason Neale, the hymnographer), at the invitation of Father Charles Fuge Lowder. The foundation was intended for Mission work in Father Lowder's parish of London Docks, but succeeding generations felt that the Community was being called to a life of greater withdrawal, and earlier this century the Benedictine Office, and later the Rule of St Benedict, were adopted.

The Community aims to achieve the Benedictine balance of prayer, study and work. All the work, whether manual, artistic or intellectual, is done within the Enclosure. The daily celebrations of the Eucharist and the Divine Office are the centre and inspiration of all activity.

Apart from worship, prayer and intercession, and the work of maintaining the house, garden and grounds, the Community's works are: the publications and greetings cards described below; providing retreats and quiet days; and dealing with a large postal apostolate.

SISTER MARY LUKE WISE CHC
(Mother Superior, elected 8 Nov 1991)
SISTER MARY JULIAN GOUGH CHC *(Assistant Superior)*
Sister Mary Michael Titherington
Sister Mary Bernadette Priddin
Sister Mary Laurence Bagshaw
Sister Mary Joseph Thorpe
Sister Mary Sylvia Driscall
Novices: 1

Obituaries

7 Jun 1998 Sister Mary Katharine Walsh, aged 81, professed 37 years, Mother Superior 1978-91

Community Publications

The sisters write and publish two sets of leaflets of devotional and spiritual content. One concerns *Unity between Christians* and a wider ecumenism. The other is on *Prayer and Faith,* reflecting the mission of the Church in the world. There is also an advent *Newsletter* published in early December. All are available from the Publications Secretary.

Office Book: CHC Office.

A Registered Charity.

Community History

Alan Russell, *The Community of the Holy Cross Haywards Heath 1857 - 1957: A Short History of its Life and Work,* 1957.

A leaflet: *Elizabeth Neale and the early history of CHC.*

Community Wares

A great variety of prayer and greeting cards are available for sale. Some are produced by the sisters and others are from a number of different sources.

Guest and Retreat Facilities

There is limited accommodation for residential, private retreats: main meals are taken at the Convent. The Community also provides for Quiet Days for individuals or groups up to twenty.

Oblates and Associates

The Community has women Oblates who are attached to it in a union of mutual prayers. Each has a rule of life adapted to her particular circumstances. Oblates are not Religious but they seek to live their life in the world according to the spirit of the Rule of St Benedict.

There are also Associates who have a much simpler rule.

Holy Cross Convent, Rempstone

Community of the Holy Family

CHF

Founded 1898

The Gatehouse
St Mary's Abbey
Swan Street
West Malling, Kent
ME19 6LP
UK

Tel: 01732 849016

Office Book:
An adaptation of the Anglican Office Book.

In January 1997, the community moved from Baldslow to the Gatehouse of West Malling Abbey. It is anticipated that the spirit of the educational work begun by the Foundress, Mother Agnes Mason, at the beginning of this century, will still be continued in the eastern end of the Diocese of Chichester through the Mother Agnes Trust which undergirds the Community of the Holy Family. The charity in the future will seek to provide a theological library and an extensive educational resource centre.

MOTHER KATHLEEN MARY CHF
(Mother Superior, assumed office 1992)
SISTER PHYLLIS ELLA CHF (*Assistant Superior*)
Sister Jean

Community History
Community of the Holy Family: the first sixty years 1898-1958. Privately produced & sold by the Community.

Associates
The Friends of the Holy Family.

Mattins
6.35 am (8.00 am Sun)

Eucharist
7.30 am (9.00 am Sun)
(with OSB sisters)

Terce
9.35 am (10.35 am Sun)

Midday Office
12.20 pm
(12.35 pm Sun)

Vespers
4.50 pm

Compline
7.50 pm

The Gate House, Malling Abbey, home of the CHF sisters, showing the Pilgrim Chapel (on the right) where they say the Office.

Community of the Holy Name

CHN

Founded 1888

Community House
40 Cavanagh Street
Cheltenham
Victoria 3192
AUSTRALIA

Tel: 03 9583 2087
Fax: 03 9585 2932

Eucharist
7.30 am
(5.30 pm Mon)

Mattins
9.00 am

Midday Office
12.45 pm

Vespers
5.30 pm
(5.00 pm Mon)

Compline
8.30 pm

Office Book:
An adaptation of the Anglican Office Book

The Community of the Holy Name was founded within the Diocese of Melbourne by Emma Caroline Silcock (Sister Esther) in 1888. The work of the community was initially amongst the poor and disadvantaged in the slum areas of inner-city Melbourne.

Over the years, the Sisters have sought to maintain a balance between a ministry to those in need and a commitment to the Divine Office, personal prayer and a daily Eucharist.

Throughout much of its history, the community was involved in prison and court work, children's homes, hospitals, hostels, retreat houses, a girl's secondary school and an indigenous community in Papua New Guinea.

In these post-institution times, Sisters are now actively engaged in parishes, AIDS and drug and alcohol ministries. Chaplaincies in hospitals (both general and psychiatric) and nursing homes, as well as in spiritual direction and leading retreats.

SISTER VALMAI CHN
(*Mother Superior, assumed office 21 March 1994*)
SISTER JOSEPHINE MARGARET CHN(*Assistant Superior*)

Aileen	Hilary	Pamela
Avrill	Hilda	Philippa
Betty	Jean	Penelope
Caroline	Jennifer	Ruth
Carol	Joyce Anne	Sheila
Elizabeth Gwen	Jenny	Sheila Anne
Faye	Lois	Shirley
Felicity	Lyn	Winifred Muriel
Francine	Maree	
Gracemary	Margaret Anne	*Novices:* 1
Gwendoline	Margot	*Postulants:* 1

Other Australian Addresses

68 Pickett Street, Footscray, VIC 3011
8 Leonard Street, Heidelberg West, VIC 3081
St Julians, 33 Lorna Street, Cheltenham, VIC 3192
48 Charles Street, Lorne, VIC 3232
5 Emerald Street, South Oakleigh, VIC 3166
Bethel, 26 Friendship Square, Cheltenham, VIC 3192

Community Publication

An *Associates Letter* is published four times a year. Write to Sister Avrill, the Associates Sister, for a subscription, which is by donation.

The Community House, Cheltenham, Victoria, Australia

Community History

Sister Elizabeth CHN, *Esther, Mother Foundress,* 1948.
Lynn Strahan, *Out of the Silence,* OUP, Melbourne, 1988.

Community Wares

Cards are sold at the Community House.

Guest and Retreat Facilities

There is accommodation for five guests at the Community House. A Sister is available for help and guidance if requested.
St Julians and Bethel both take men or women in a crisis situation or needing respite accommodation.

Oblates and Associates

The Order of Oblates for women and men who desire to lead lives of prayer and dedication in close association with the Community. The Oblates have a personal Rule of Life based on the Evangelical Counsels of Poverty, Chastity and Obedience and renew their dedication annually.
The Associates and Priest Associates have a simple Rule of Life and commit themselves to pray regularly for the Community. The Priest Associates offer the Eucharist with special intention for the Community quarterly and promote the Religious Life.

* * *

EDITORS' NOTE: *The Community of the Holy Name in the UK and Africa, which forms several of the* subsequent *entries in this directory, is a community entirely distinct from CHN in Australia. Although sharing the same name, the two communities were founded independently of each other.*

Community of the Holy Name

(UK Province)

CHN

Founded 1865

Convent of the Holy Name
Morley Road
Oakwood
Derby DE21 4QZ
UK

Tel: 01332 671716
Fax: 01332 669712

Prime
7.45 am (8.15 am Tue)

Eucharist
8.00 am
(12.20 pm Tue & Thu)

Mattins
9.15 am
(8.45 am Thu, 9.30 am Sun)

Midday Office
12.45 pm
(12.05 pm Tue & Thu)

Vespers
5.00 pm

Compline
9.15 pm
(8.00 pm Sat)

Office Book:
Daily Office CHN

Registered Charity:
No. 250256

The Sisters combine the life of prayer with service to others in their evangelistic and pastoral outreach and by maintaining their houses as centres of prayer where they can be available to others. They run a retreat house and conference centre in Chester (until December 2000), a small guest house in Derby, and are able to take one or two guests in the house at Keswick. In other houses, and from the Convent in Derby, the Sisters are involved in parish work, prison visiting, retreat-giving and work among some who are disabled, and those who come for counselling.

The members of the Fellowship of the Holy Name are an extension of its life and witness in the world.

MOTHER JEAN MARY CHN
(Provincial Superior, assumed office 14 January 1994)
SISTER MONICA JANE CHN *(Assistant Superior)*

Sister Barbara Mary
Sister Michael
Sister Colette
Sister Mary Sethrid
Sister Christian
Sister Penelope
Sister Judith
Sister Ruth
Sister Mary Janet
Sister Mary Alison
Sister Francesca Mary
Sister Sheila Margaret
Sister Nikola
Sister Marjorie Jean
Sister Mariette
Sister Mary Ruth
Sister Barbara
Sister Gladys Mary
Sister Joy
Sister Elizabeth Rachel
Sister Brenda
Sister Verena
Sister Constance
Sister Lilias
Sister Marjorie Eileen
Sister Jessica Mary
Sister Theresa Margaret
Sister Mary Patricia
Sister Beryl
Sister Lisbeth
Sister Vivienne Joy
Sister Charity
Sister Renate
Sister Elizabeth Clare
Sister Vivienne
Sister Diana
Sister Edith Margaret
Sister Dorothy
Sister Pauline Margaret
Sister Pamela
Sister Carol
Sister Pippa
Sister Rosemary
Sister Irene
Sister Lynfa
Sister Elaine Mary
Sister Julie Elizabeth
Novices: 4

Society of the Holy Trinity: Sister Rosemary SHT

Obituaries

24 Dec 1998	Sister Bernardine, aged 65, professed 31 years
8 Jan 1999	Sister Dorothy Helen, aged 89, professed 27 years

Other UK houses

The Retreat House
11 Abbey Square
Chester
CH1 2HU
Tel: 01244 321801
(until December 2000)

88 Braunston Road
Oakham
Rutland
LE15 6LE
Tel: 01572 770287

Holy Name House
Ambleside Road
Keswick
Cumbria
CA12 4DD
Tel: 01768 772998

Cottage 5
Lambeth Palace
London
SE1 7JU
Tel: 0207 928 5407

6 St Peter's Court
398 Woodborough
Road
Nottingham
NG3 4JF
Tel: 0115 9608794

64 Allexton Gardens
Welland Estate
Peterborough
PE1 4UW
Tel: 01733 352077

St Michael's
53 Wimborne Road
Radford
Nottingham
NG7 5PD
Tel: 0115 9785101

The Convent of the Holy Name, Derby

Community History

History of the Community of the Holy Name, 1865 to 1950, published by CHN, 1950.
Portrait of a Community, Church Army Press, 1972.

Community Wares

Candles, recycled cards and hand-painted cards, as well as prayer stones (either painted or with a Celtic design) are all for sale at the Convent (but not through the post).

Guest and Retreat Facilities

There are opportunities for individuals to make a private retreat at the guest house, and Sisters would be prepared to give help and guidance if requested. We do not organise group retreats.

Fellowship of the Holy Name

The Fellowship is comprised of ecumenically-minded Christians who feel called to share with the Community in their life of prayer and service.

Members have a personal Rule of Life, which they have drawn up in consultation with a particular Sister. She will keep in contact and help with a regular review. This rule will include daily private prayer, regular prayer and worship with the local Christian community, as well as time and space for their own well-being and creativity. Each rule varies with the individual. A six-month probation living the rule is required before formal admission to the Fellowship. This usually takes place at the Convent in the context of the Eucharist. There are regional meetings for members living in the same area, and the Community distributes a quarterly magazine comprised of articles submitted by members.

Community of the Holy Name (Lesotho Province)

CHN

Founded 1865 (in UK)
1962 (in Lesotho)

Convent of the Holy Name
PO Box LR43
Leribe
LESOTHO

Tel: 4000249

Morning Prayer 6.30 am (6.45 am Sun)

Terce

7.45 am (Sun only)

Eucharist

7.00 am (8.00 am Sun; 12 noon Wed)

Midday Office
12.15 pm (12.30 pm Sun, 11.45 am Wed)

Evening Prayer 5.00 pm

Compline 8.15 pm

Office Book:
South African Prayer Book, supplemented by the CHN Office Book (using both Sesotho & English)

The Basotho Community of S. Mary at the Cross was founded in Leribe, Lesotho, in 1923, under the Community of St Michael & All Angels, Bloemfontein. In 1959, CHN Sisters were invited to take over this work and started at Leribe in 1962. They had invited the Sisters of S. Mary at the Cross to become members of CHN and the full amalgamation of the two communities was completed in 1964. As a multi-racial community, the witness against racism at a time when apartheid was in the ascendant in South Africa was an important strand of the Community's vocation. New members have joined the Community in succeeding years, and they have continued the evangelistic and pastoral work which is also an important part of the CHN vocation. Sisters are involved in youth work, prison visiting, as well as helping in both Lesotho and South Africa.

This work is enabled and strengthened by the daily round of prayer, both corporate and private, which is at the heart of the Community's Rule. A daily Eucharist at the centre of this life of prayer is the aim, but in some houses this is not always possible owing to a shortage of priests.

Ten Sisters in Leribe run a hostel for secondary school students who live too far from home to travel daily.

SISTER LUCIA CHN
(*Sister Provincial, elected December 1995*)
SISTER MARIA CHN (*Assistant Superior*)

Sister Calista
Sister Alphonsina
Sister Hilda Tsepiso
Sister Frangeni
Sister Francina
Sister Elizabetha
Sister Angelina
Sister Mary Selina
Sister Josetta
Sister Lerato Maria

Sister Jemima
Sister Veronica Mpolokeng
Sister Angela Tsoana
Sister Gertrude
Sister Ryneth
Sister Julia
Sister Lineo

Novices: 2

Other House

CHN Mission House, Po Box 7142, Maseru, LESOTHO

Community Wares

Church sewing (including cassocks, albs & stoles); communion wafers; Mothers Union & school uniforms;mohair and woven goods from the Leribe Craft Centre and the disabled workshop, started by the Community.

Community of the Holy Name (Zulu Province)

CHN

Founded 1865 (in UK)
1969 (in Zululand)

Convent of the Holy Name
Pt. Bag 806
Melmoth
Zululand
SOUTH AFRICA

Tel: 3545 2892

Mattins
6.30 am

Eucharist
7.00 am (Tues, Wed, Thurs; 12 noon Fri)

Terce
8.30 am

Midday Office
12.30 pm (11.45 am Fri)

Evening Prayer
5.00 pm

Compline
7.45 pm

Office Book:
Offices are mainly in Zulu, based on the South African Prayer Book & the CHN Office Book.

The Community of the Holy Name in Zululand was founded by three Zulu Sisters who began their Religious Life with the Community in Leribe. All three Provinces of CHN have the same Rule of life, but there are differences of customary and constitutions to fit in with cultural differences. The daily life of the Community centres around the daily Office, and the Eucharist whenever the presence of a priest makes this possible.

The Sisters are involved extensively in mission, pastoral and evangelistic work. The Zulu Sisters have evangelistic gifts which are used in parishes throughout the diocese at the invitation of parish priests. Several Sisters have trained as teachers or nurses. They work in schools or hospitals, where possible within reach of one of the Community houses. Their salaries, and the handicrafts on sale at the Convent at Kwa Magwaza, help to keep the Community solvent.

MOTHER OLPHA CHN
(*Provincial Superior, elected January 1996*)
SISTER CLAUDIA CHN (*Assistant Superior*)

Sister Gertrude Jabulisiwe
Sister Nesta Gugu
Sister Victoria Nokuthula
Sister Sibongile
Sister Zodwa
Sister Mantombi
Sister Bonakele
Sister Nonhlahla
Sister Jabu
Sister Sibusisiwe
Sister Thulisiwe
Sister Lindiwe
Sister Happiness
Sister Gloria
Sister Nomusa
Sister Ntombi
Sister Sebenzile
Sister Thembelihla
Sister Benzile
Sister Samkelisiwe
Sister Thandazile
Sister Nondumiso
Sister Ethel
Sister Thokozile
Sister Duduzile
Sister Patricia
Sister Phindile
Sister Grace
Sister Nqobile
Sister Gladys
Sister Dumisile
Sister Makhosazana
Sister Cynthia
Sister Sibekezelo
Sister Xolisile
Sister Philisiwe
Sister Ntsoaki
Sister Nomphumeleo
Sister Nokubongwa
Sister Nozibusiso
Sister Beauty
Sister Thandukwazi
Sister Nomathemba
Sister Aurelia
Sister Zamandla
Sister Sindisiwe
Sister Agnetta
Sister Nkosingiphile
Sister Somkazi
Sister Bongile

Novices: 4

Other Houses

St Vincent's Mission
P/B 675
Nqutu 3135
Natal
SOUTH AFRICA

Usuthu Mission
PO Luyengo
SWAZILAND

Mission House of the Holy Name
14 Web Castle Way
Castle Hill
Marble Ray
Durban 4037
SOUTH AFRICA

St Luke's Mission
PO Box 175
3950 Nongoma
SOUTH AFRICA

c/o Rt Revd J. Dlamini
PO Box 163
Umtata, Transkei
SOUTH AFRICA

Community Wares
Vestments, cassocks, albs and other forms of dressmaking to order.

Community of Jesus' Compassion

CJC

Founded 1992

PO Box 153
New Hanover
3230
SOUTH AFRICA

Founded in the Diocese of Natal by a sister from the Community of the Holy Name in Zululand, CJC have been based in several locations. However, the sisters have now settled at New Hanover, which is half an hour's drive from the cathedral city of Pietermaritzburg. The main work of the sisters is evangelising in the local parish.

On the 19th December 1998, the first life professions within the community were received, prior to the Community's formal recognition by the Church of the Province of South Africa.

SISTER LONDIWE CJC
(*Foundress*)
Sister Thandi
Sister Yeki
Sister Zandile
Sister Philisiwe
Sister Jabulile
Sister Ntombi
Sister Nontokozo
Sister Thokozile
Sister Nqobile
Sister S'bongile
Sister Hlengiwe
Sister Phumzile
Sister Nonhlanhla

Community of Nazareth

CN

Founded 1936

4-22-30 Mure
Mitaka
Tokyo 181-0002
JAPAN

Tel: 0422 48 4560
Fax: 0422 48 4601

Morning Prayer
5.55 am

Eucharist
7.00 am

Terce
8.15 am

Sext
12 noon

None
after lunch

Evening Prayer
5.00 pm

Night Prayer
8.15 pm

Office Book:
BCP of Nippon Seiko Kai
Office Book

Under the guidance of the Sisters of the Community of the Epiphany (England), the Community of Nazareth was born and has grown. The Community is dedicated to the Incarnate Lord Jesus Christ, especially in devotion to the hidden life which he lived in Nazareth.

In addition to the Holy Eucharist, which is the centre and focus of our community life, the Sisters recite a sixfold Divine Office.

We run a Retreat house and make wafers and vestments.

We welcome enquirers and aspirants.

SISTER MIYOSHI CN
(*Revd Mother, assumed office 23 March 1996*)
SISTER CHIZUKO CN (*Assistant Mother*)

Sister Yachiyo
Sister Chiyo
Sister Haruko
Sister Kayoko
Sister Nobu
Sister Asako
Sister Setsuko
Sister Yukie
Sister Junko
Sister Sachiko
Sister Kazuko

Obituaries
10 Aug 1998 Sister Shizue, aged 82, professed 43 years

Other House

81 Shima Bukuro
Naka Gusuku Son
Naka Gami Gun
Okinawa Ken 9012301
JAPAN

Community Wares
Wafers, vestments, postcards.

Guest and Retreat Facilities
There are twenty rooms available, for men or women, but not children. The suggested donation is ¥6,000 per night, including three meals. The Retreat House is closed for two weeks after Christmas.

Associates
Clergy and laity may be associates.

Community of the Resurrection

CR

Founded 1892

House of the Resurrection
Mirfield
West Yorkshire
WF14 0BN
UK
Tel: 01924 494318
Fax: 01924 490489
E-Mail:
cr@mirfield.org.uk

Mattins
6.45 am (7.15 am Thu, 7.30 am Sun)

Mass
follows Mattins (12.30 pm Thu, 8.00 am Sun)

Midday Office
12.45 pm
(12.15 pm Thu)

Evensong
7.00 pm (6.30 pm Sun)

Compline
9.45 pm

Office Book:
CR Office

Registered Charity:
No. 232670

The Community consists of priests and laymen living together as brothers a life devoted to prayer and worship, work and study. They undertake a wide range of pastoral ministry, both in the UK and South Africa. Their work includes a theological college at Mirfield and retreat houses, together with evangelism and counselling.

CRISPIN HARRISON CR
(assumed office 6 January 1998)
WILLIAM NICOL CR *(Prior)*

Dominic Whitnall	Simon Holden
Luke Smith	Christopher Lowe
Anselm Genders *(bishop)*	Jonathan Critchley
Roy France	Harry Williams
Timothy Stanton	Antony Grant
Aelred Stubbs	David Wilson
Vincent Girling	Nicolas Stebbing
Kingston Erson	John Gribben
Clifford Green	Peter Allan
Zachary Brammer	Andrew Norton
Benedict Green	George Guiver
Alexander Cox	Philip Nichols
Eric Simmons	Thomas Seville
Aidan Mayoss	Patrick Souter
Silvanus Berry	
Robert Mercer *(bishop)*	*Novices:* 2

Obituaries

20 Apr 1998	Trevor Huddleston *(bishop)*, aged 84, professed 56 years
14 Jun 1998	Benjamin Baynham, aged 86, professed 54 years

Other addresses

St Michael's Priory, 14 Burleigh Street, London WC2E 7PX, UK
Tel: 0207 379 6669 *Fax: 0207 240 5294*
E-Mail: amayoss@mirfield.org.uk

St Peter's Priory, PO Box 991, Southdale 2135, SOUTH AFRICA *Tel: 11 434 2504* *Fax: 11 434 4556*
E-Mail: crpriory@ acunet.co.za

Community Publication

CR Quarterly. Write to the Director FR at the House of the Resurrection.

Community History

Alan Wilkinson, *The Community of the Resurrection: A centenary history*, SCM Press, London, 1992.

Community Wares
Postcards of the House, leaflets on prayer: apply to Mirfield Publications at the House of the Resurrection.

Guest and Retreat Facilities
Retreats are listed in *Retreats* (formerly *Vision*).
HOUSE OF THE RESURRECTION
Twenty single rooms, two double rooms. Apply to the Guestmaster.

Most convenient time to telephone: 9.00 am - 12.30 pm, 2.00 pm - 6.30 pm

A further retreat house, owned but not staffed by CR, is:
ST FRANCIS' HOUSE, Hemingford Grey, Huntingdon, Cambs., PE18 9BJ, UK
Tel: 01480 462185
Seventeen single rooms, three twin rooms. Apply to the Warden.

COLLEGE OF THE RESURRECTION *Principal: The Revd Christopher Irving*
The College, founded in 1902, trains men for ordination to the priesthood and also provides opportunities for men and women to study for degrees at the University of Leeds.

College of the Resurrection, Mirfield, West Yorkshire WF14 0BW, UK
Tel: 01924 490441 *Fax: 01924 492738* *E-Mail: cirvine@mirfield.org.uk*

MIRFIELD CENTRE
The Centre offers a meeting place at the College for about fifty people. Small residential conferences are possible in the summer vacation. Day and evening events are arranged throughout the year to stimulate Christian life and witness.

The Mirfield Centre (College of the Resurrection), Mirfield, West Yorkshire WF14 0BW, UK
Tel: 01924 481920 *Fax: 01924 492738* *E-Mail: centre@mirfield.org.uk*

Fraternity of the Resurrection
The Fraternity is an integral part of the family of the Community of the Resurrection. There are four categories of membership:

1. OBLATES
These are priests and laymen who accept a vocation to live their lives according to the evangelical counsels of poverty, chastity and obedience.

2. COMPANIONS
These are men and women, clerical and lay, who are joined to the Community in a rule of worship, study and service.

3. ASSOCIATES
These are those who wish for a less demanding link with the Community, or who already have a comparable relationship with another Community.

4. FRIENDS
These are Christians or members of another faith or of none who consider that while the obligations of Eucharistic worship are not for them, they are nevertheless interested in the Community.

Community of the Resurrection of Our Lord

CR

Founded 1884

PO Box 72
Grahamstown 6140
SOUTH AFRICA

Tel & Fax:
046 622 4210

Morning Office
6.30 am

Eucharist
7.00 am
(at the Cathedral Mon & Wed)

Midday Office
12.30 pm

Corporate intercession
5.30 pm

Evening Office
5.45 pm
(Prayer Book)

Compline
After supper, in house groups or privately.

Office Book:
An Anglican Prayer Book of the CPSA;
Traditional Midday Office & Compline.

This Community was founded in 1884 by Bishop Allan Becher Webb and Cecile Isherwood to undertake pastoral and educational work in Grahamstown. These two types of work, and later Social Welfare work, have predominated in the Community's undertakings throughout its history. The regular life of monastic Offices and personal prayer and intercession has always been maintained, both in the Mother House (Grahamstown) and all branch houses, wherever situated. It is still maintained in Grahamstown, the only centre where the Community life continues, our numbers being now much reduced, with a high proportion of elderly and infirm members.

Two Retreat Centres established by this Community have been taken over by other Communities: St Peter's Bourne in north London is now run by CSMV (Wantage), and Hillandale, near Grahamstown, has recently been taken over by the Order of the Holy Cross, an Anglican Benedictine community for men, based in the USA.

Two schools, staffed entirely by lay teachers, remain under the management of the Grahamstown Community.

MOTHER CAROL CR
(Mother Superior, assumed office 13 November 1998)

Sister Evelyn
Sister Heloise
Sister Felicity
Sister Dorianne
Sister Mary Brigid
Sister Nonie
Sister Joyce Mary
Sister Jean Mary
Sister Erica
Sister Judith
Sister Prisca
Sister Kathleen Mary
Sister Moira
Sister Paulina
Sister Edwina
Sister Zelma

Obituaries

1 Aug 1998 — Sister Mariya, aged 84, professed 59 years
3 Oct 1998 — Sister Truda, aged 95, professed 55 years

Community Publication

A Newsletter is sent out to all Bishops and Religious Communities of CPSA, and also to all Oblates and Associates of the Community, two or three times a year.

Community History

A pictorial record of the Community's history, with commentary, was published in its centenary year, 1984. It was a colloborative work.

Lives of Mother Cecile and her successor, Mother Florence, have been published, in each case written by 'a Sister':

A Sister of the Community (compiler), *Mother Cecile in South Africa 1883-1906: Foundress of the Community of the Resurrection of Our Lord*, SPCK, London, 1930
A Sister of the Community, *The Story of a Vocation: A Brief Memoir of Mother Florence, Second Superior of the Community of the Resurrection of Our Lord*, The Church Book Shop, Grahamstown, no date.

Community Wares
Cards, banners and three-point stoles.

Guest and Retreat Facilities
Three or four guests can be accommodated; though prior consultation is needed. The charge is negotiable.

Oblates and Associates
OBLATES OF THE RISEN CHRIST live under a Rule drawn up for each individual according to circumstances, on their observance of which they must report monthly to the Oblate Sister.
ASSOCIATES undertake a simple Rule, including regular prayer for the Community.
FRIENDS are interested in the Community and pray for it, and keep in touch with it.

Community of the Sacred Passion

CSP

Founded 1911

The Convent of the Sacred Passion
Lower Road
Effingham
Leatherhead
Surrey
KT24 5JP
UK
Tel: 01372 457091

Morning Prayer
7.10 am

Mass
7.30 am
(Mon. Tue. Wed. Fri)

Prayer before noon
8.40 am

Midday Office
12.10 pm

Evening Prayer
6.00 pm

Compline
8.45 pm

Office Book:
Daily Prayer

Registered Charity:
No. 800080

The Community was founded to serve Africa by a life of prayer and missionary work. Prayer is the centre of the life of the Community and all activity flows from it. The Mother House is now in England. The Community withdrew from Africa in 1991, leaving behind the Tanzanian Community of St Mary of Nazareth & Calvary, which they had founded (see separate entry, page 31).

The way the sisters live out their vocation depends on local circumstances. At Effingham, guests are welcomed for times of quiet and private retreat. Visiting the sick and house-bound and prison, cathedral and hospital chaplaincy work are also undertaken. Walsall often has visitors. In this house, sisters give help in the parishes which includes visiting, speaking, conducting retreats, hospital and industrial chaplaincy, and inter-faith dialogue. A small group of sisters live next to the St Julian's Shrine in Norwich. Here, the main ministry is hospitality to visitors to the Shrine.

MOTHER PHILIPPA CSP
(Mother Superior, assumed office 30 August 1999)

Sister Stella
Sister Greta
Sister Felicitas
Sister Olive Marian
Sister Gloria
Sister Etheldreda
Sister Mary Columba
Sister Jean Margaret
Sister Dorothy
Sister Thelma Mary
Sister Mary Joan
Sister Ruby
Sister Joan Thérèse
Sister Gillian Mary
Sister Rhoda
Sister Mary Stella
Sister Angela
Sister Jacqueline
Sister Joy
Sister Lucia
Sister Mary Kathleen
Sister Mary Margaret
Sister Phoebe

Obituaries

19 May 1998	Sister Joanna Mary, aged 83, professed 46 years
6 Oct 1998	Sister Rose Mary, aged 90, professed 62 years
1 Aug 1999	Sister Blandina, aged 88, professed 52 years

Other Houses

The Convent
14 Laing House
Walstead Road
Walsall WS5 4NJ
UK
Tel: 01922 644267

All Hallows House
St Julian's Alley
Rouen Road
Norwich NRI 1QT
UK
Tel: 01603 624738

Community History
Sister Mary Stella CSP, *She Won't Say 'No': The History of the Community of the Sacred Passion,* privately published, 1984.

Guest and Retreat Facilities
Private retreatants are welcome in the small guest house at Effingham.

Oblates
These are men and women who feel called to associate themselves with the aims of the community, by prayer and service, and by a life under a Rule. They have their own Rule of Life which will vary according to their particular circumstances. The Oblates are helped and advised by the Mistress of Oblates.

Associates
These are men and women who share in the work of the community by prayer, almsgiving and service of some kind. They pray regularly for the community.

Priest Associates
They pray regularly for the community and offer Mass for it three times a year, of which one is Passion Sunday (the Sunday before Palm Sunday).

Friends
They pray regularly for the community and help it in any way they can.

All those connected with the community are prayed for daily by the Sisters and remembered by name on their birthdays. They receive the four monthly intercession paper.

The Chapel, CSP, Effingham

Community of St Andrew

CSA

Founded 1861

St Andrew's House
2 Tavistock Road
Westbourne Park
London
W11 1BA
UK

Tel: 0207 229 2662
Fax: 0207 792 5993

Morning Prayer
7.30 am
7.10 am (Mon & Wed)
8.00 am (Sat)

Eucharist
7.30 am (Mon & Wed)
9.30 am (Tue)
12.30 pm (Thu & Fri)

Midday Prayer
12.45 pm
1.15 pm (Sun)
12.15 pm (Thu & Fri)

Evening Prayer
6.00 pm

Night Prayer
9.00 pm

Office Book:
Celebrating Common Prayer

Registered Charity:
No. 244321

Full membership of the Community consists of Professed Sisters who are ordained, or who, though not seeking ordination, serve in other forms of diaconal ministry, such as the caring professions. The fundamental ministry is the offering of prayer and worship, evangelism, pastoral work and hospitality. This is carried out through parish and specialised ministry.

MOTHER DONELLA CSA *(deacon)*
(Mother Superior, assumed office 13 Oct 1994)
SISTER DENZIL CSA *(priest) (Assistant Superior)*

Sister Joan *(deacon)*
Sister Hilary *(deacon)*
Sister Eleanor *(deaconess)*
Sister Dorothy *(deaconess)*
Sister Pamela *(deaconess)*
Sister Lillian *(deacon)*
Sister Patricia *(deacon)* *(Novice Guardian)*
Sister Teresa *(priest)*

Obituaries

30 Apr 1998 Sister Julian *(priest)*, aged 78, professed 41 years
13 Nov 1998 Sister Barbara *(deaconess)*, aged 90, professed 51 years

Community Publications

St Andrew's Review & *St Andrew's Newsletter*. Write to the Revd Mother CSA.
Distinctive Diaconate & *Distinctive News of Women in Ministry*, both edited by Revd Sister Teresa CSA.

Guest and Retreat Facilities

Guest rooms, and facilities for individual or group quiet days. One room for residential (individually-guided or private) retreat.

Associates

Our Associates are part of our extended Community family. They may be men, women, clergy or lay, and follow a simple Rule of Life, which includes praying for the Sisters and their work. Friends are also part of our fellowship of prayer and support the Sisters in many ways.

The Sisters pray for the Associates and Friends every day and also arrange special retreats, quiet days, and social gatherings for them every year, and can be available to give help or guidance if required.

Community of St Clare

OSC

Founded 1950

St Mary's Convent
178 Wroslyn Road
Freeland
Witney
Oxfordshire
OX8 8AJ
UK

Tel: 01993 881225
Fax: 01993 882434

Office of Readings
5.30 am

Morning Prayer
7.00 am

Eucharist
8.30 am

Midday Prayer
12.00 noon

Evening Prayer
5.00 pm

Night Prayer
8.15 pm

Office Book:
The Daily Office SSF

The Community of St Clare is part of the Society of St Francis. We are a group of women who live together needing each other's help to give our whole lives to the worship of God. Our service to the world is by our prayer, in which we are united with all people everywhere. We have a guest house so that others may join in our worship, and share the quiet and beauty with which we are surrounded. We try to provide for our own needs by growing much of our own food, and by our work of printing, wafer baking, writing and various crafts. This also helps us to have something material to share with those in greater need.

Sister Paula Fordham OSC
(Abbess, elected 7 May 1997)
Sister Alison Francis Hamilton OSC *(Deputy Leader)*

Sister Elsie Felicity Watts
Sister Patricia Wighton
Sister Gillian Clare Amies
Sister Mary Margaret Broomfield
Sister Susan Elisabeth Leslie
Sister Damian Davies
Sister Michaela Davis
Sister Mary Kathleen Kearns
Sister Elizabeth Farley
Sister Christine Julian Fraser

Community Wares
Printing, cards, crafts, altar breads.
Tel & Fax to Print Shop: 01993 882434

Guest and Retreat Facilities
Men, women and children are welcome at the guest house. It is not a 'silent house' but people can make private retreats if they wish. Please write to the Guest Sister at the Convent address.

Most convenient time to telephone: 6.00 pm - 7.00 pm

Address of the Guest House (for guests arriving)
The Old Parsonage
168 Wroslyn Road
Freeland
Oxford OX8 8AQ
UK
Tel: 01993 881227

Community of St Denys

CSD

Founded 1879

St Denys Retreat Centre
2/3 Church Street
Warminster BA12 8PG
UK

Tel: 01985 214824

Timetable of Sisters' Chapel at the Retreat House:

Morning Prayer
7.15 am

Midday Prayer
12.30 pm

Evening Prayer & Eucharist
5.00 pm

Compline
Time varies

Office Book: Celebrating Common Prayer

A Registered Charity.

The Community was founded in 1879 for mission work at home and overseas. We now fulfil our calling as a dispersed community engaged in adult teaching, parish work, spiritual guidance and retreat work.

There are two houses in Warminster in addition to the Retreat House. Sisters also live in Salisbury, Wilts, and Barking in Essex. All enquiries should be sent to the Leader c/o the Retreat House.

REVD MOTHER FRANCES ANNE COCKER CSD *(priest)*
(Mother Superior, assumed office 27 Jun 1987)
SISTER ELIZABETH MARY NOLLER CSD (*priest*)
(*Assistant Superior*)
Sister Ruth Gunnery
Sister Stephanie Steppat *(priest)*
Sister Doris Spruce
Sister Carol Ham
Sister Gladys Henbest
Sister Julian Buggy
Sister Christine Hudson
Sister Eileen Fryer
Sister Margaret Mary Powell
Sister Phyllis Urwin
Novices: 1

Obituaries
23 July 1999 Sister Jennetta Richardson, aged 102, professed 68 years

Other addresses

Revd Mother CSD
Sarum College
19 The Close
Salisbury SP1 2EE
UK
Tel: 01722 339761

Church Flat
St Margaret's Centre
The Broadway
Barking
Essex IG11 8AS
UK
Tel: 0208 594 1736
(evenings only)

Community Publication
Annual *Newsletter* and quarterly prayer leaflet. Write to the Secretary of the S. Denys Fellowship, 2/3 Church St, Warminster, Wilts BA12 8PG, UK. The suggested donation is £5.00 per annum.

Community History
CSD: The Life & Work of St Denys', Warminster to 1979, published by CSD, 1979.

Community Wares
Recycled cards for charities.

Guest and Retreat Facilities
ST DENYS RETREAT CENTRE is available for various types of retreat and parish conferences. Guests are also welcome. It has twenty-two rooms, six of which are double. The Centre is closed at Christmas (except to Oblates and relatives of Sisters).

The Sisters lead 'Walk-in to quietness with God' days, Individually-Guided Retreats and traditional preached Retreats, both in Warminster and elsewhere.

Apply to the Retreat Sceretary for further details.

Most convenient time to telephone: 10.00 am - 12 noon, 6.45 pm - 8.00 pm

Oblates and Associates
CSD has oblates, associates (ordained and lay), and a fellowship (i.e. friends). There have been resident oblates in the past, although there are none at present.

****

CSF sisters in the chapel at Compton Durville
(see next page)

Community of St Francis

CSF

Founded 1905

UK Houses

43 Endymion Road
Brixton
London SW2 2BU
Tel: 0208 671 9401

Minister Provincial
Tel & Fax:
0208 674 5344
E-Mail: Joycecsf@aol.com

St Francis House
113 Gillott Rd
Birmingham
B16 0ET
Tel: 0121 454 8302
Fax 0121 455 9784
E-Mail: hilary@
csfbham.swinternet.co.uk

This autonomous Community is part of the Society of St Francis: the First Order Sisters. Sisters are engaged in spiritual direction and evangelistic and caring ministry, sometimes alongside brothers of the Society. Some part-time salaried work is necessary to help generate income. Guests are received in all houses of the Community; in some, there is space for retreatants and other groups. The Eucharist is central to the Community's life and is celebrated regularly in all houses.

TERESA CSF
(Minister General, assumed office 7 Feb 1996)

EUROPEAN PROVINCE

JOYCE CSF
(Minister Provincial, assumed office 30 July 1996)

Alison Mary	Jennie
Angela Helen	Judith Ann
Beverley	Maureen
Chris	Moyra
Christine James	Nan
Elizabeth	Patricia Clare
Gina	Phyllis
Gwenfryd Mary	Rose
Helen Julian	Rowan Clare
Hilary	Sue
Jackie	Veronica
Jannafer	*Novices:* 1

Obituaries

17 May 1998	Angela Mary, aged 91, professed 38 years
1 Jul 1998	Barbara, aged 83, professed 32 years
10 Mar 1999	Gabriel, aged 86, professed 36 years

Community History

Elizabeth CSF, *Corn of Wheat,* Becket Publications, Oxford, 1981.

Community Publication

franciscan (published by SSF sisters and brothers), three times a year. Subscription: £4.50 per year. Write to The Editor of f*ranciscan*, The Friary, Hilfield, Dorchester, Dorset DT2 7BE, UK.

Guest and Retreat Facilities

COMPTON DURVILLE Guests are welcome, both men and women, in groups or as individuals. There are fourteen

St Francis Convent
Compton Durville
South Petherton
Somerset TA13 5ES
Tel: 01460 240473
& 241248
Fax: 01460 242360

Greystones St Francis
First Avenue
Porthill
Newcastle-under-Lyme
Staffs ST5 8QX
Tel: 01782 636839

Minister General
Tel & Fax:
01782 611180

10 Halcrow Street
Stepney
London E1 2EP
Tel: 0207 247 6233

Office Book:
The Daily Office SSF

Registered Charity:
No. 286615

single rooms and two twin-bedded. Day groups of thirty can be accommodated. A programme is available from the Guest Sister.

Third Order

The Third Order of the Society of St Francis consists of men and women, ordained and lay, married or single, who believe that God is calling them to live out their Franciscan vocation in the world, living in their own homes and doing their own jobs. Living under a rule of life, with the help of a spiritual director, members (called tertiaries) encourage one another in living and witnessing to Christ, being organised in local groups to enable regular meetings to be held. It is international in scope, with a Minister General and five Ministers Provincial to cover the relevant Provinces (see page 142 for addresses).

Companions

Companions are individual Christians who wish to associate themselves with the Society through prayer, friendship and in seeking to live the spirit of the Gospel in the way of St Francis. For more information about becoming a Companion contact: The Secretary for Companions, Hilfield Friary, Dorchester, Dorset DT2 7BE, UK.

AMERICAN PROVINCE

USA house

St Francis House
3743 Cesar Chavez Street
San Francisco
CA 94110
Tel: 415 824 0288
Fax: 415 826 7569
E-Mail: csf@sfo.com

Office Book:
CSF Office Book

PAMELA CLARE CSF
(*Minister Provincial*)

Catherine Joy	Jean
Cecilia	Ruth
Elizabeth Ann	

Guest and Retreat Facilities

At the San Francisco house, there is a guest apartment, which has one bedroom (two beds) and a small kitchen. It has its own entrance. There is no telephone. The suggested cost is $35 per night.

Community of St John Baptist (UK)

CSJB

Founded 1852

Convent of St John Baptist
Hatch Lane
Clewer, Windsor
Berkshire SL4 3QR
UK

Tel: 01753 850618
Fax: 01753 869989
E-Mail:
csjbclewer@dial.pipex.com

Lauds
7.30 am

Tierce
9.00 am
(8.45 am Sun & major feasts)

Eucharist
9.10 am
(9.00 am Sun & major feasts)

Midday Office
12.00 noon

Vespers
5.30 pm

Compline
8.45 pm
(8.15 pm Sun)

Founded by Harriet Monsell and Thomas Thelluson Carter to help women rejected by the rest of society, we are now a Community of women who seek to offer our gifts to God in varying ways. These include parish and retreat work, spiritual direction, and ministry to the elderly, to those with learning disabilities and to the marginalised. One Sister is currently training for the ordained ministry. Our links abroad include a relationship with the Sisters of our affiliated Community at Mendham, New Jersey, and two Sisters have recently visited Bangladesh.

Daily life centres around the Eucharist and the Divine Office, and we live under the threefold vows of poverty, chastity and obedience. Following the Rule of St Augustine, we are encouraged to grow into 'an ever-deepening commitment of love for God and for each other as we strive to show forth the attractiveness of Christ to the world'.

Our Oblates and Associates answer a call to prayer and service, while remaining at home and work. This calls includes a commitment to the spiritual life and active church membership. Oblates, Associates and Friends support the Sisters by prayer and in other ways, thereby making up the extended family of CSJB.

MOTHER JANE OLIVE CSJB
(Reverend Mother Superior, installed 19 August 1992)
SISTER ZOE CSJB *(Assistant Superior)*

Sister Letitia	Sister Monica
Sister Margaret	Sister Elizabeth Jane
Sister Moira	Sister Pamela
Sister Sheila	Sister Veronica Joan
Sister Doreen	Sister Mary Stephen
Sister Edna Frances	Sister Anne

Community of Reparation to Jesus in the Blessed Sacrament:
Sister Esther Mary CRJBS

Obituaries
21 Sep 1998 Sister Gladys Mary, aged 90, professed 59 years

Community Publication
Associates' Letter, three times a year.

Community Wares
Church embroidery room: vestments, etc.
Cards, books, ribbon markers.

Website: http://www.csjbclewer.org.uk

Office Book:
CSJB Office

Registered Charity:
No. 236939

Community History
Books by Valerie Bonham, all published by CSJB:
A Joyous Service: The Clewer Sisters and their Work (1989)
A Place in Life: The House of Mercy 1849-1883 (1992)
The Sisters of the Raj: The Clewer Sisters in India (1997)

Guest and Retreat Facilities
CLEWER SPIRITUALITY CENTRE: the Community welcomes groups or individuals for retreats, conferences, quiet days, parish weekends, etc. Chapels, three spacious sitting rooms, two with libraries, two dining rooms, large garden, twenty-eight single rooms, four twin-bedded. All visitors are invited to share in the worship of the Community. Maximum for resident groups, thirty-six; non-resident, forty-five. Apply to the Administrator / Warden.

Most convenient time to telephone: 9.00 am - 5.00 pm, Monday to Saturday.

Oblates & Associates
CSJB has women oblates. Men and women may become Associates or members of the Friends of Clewer.

Community of St John Baptist (USA)

CSJB

Founded 1852 (in UK)
1874 (in USA)

PO Box 240 -
82 W. Main Street
Mendham
NJ 07945
USA

Tel: 973 543 4641
Fax: 973 543 0327
E-Mail:
csjb@worldnet.att.net
Website:
http://home.att.net/~csjb/

The Community of St John Baptist was founded in England in 1852. The spirit of the Community is to "prepare the way of the Lord and make straight in the desert a highway for our God." We follow the call of our patron through a life of worship, community, and service.

Our Community is made up of monastic women, who share life together under the traditional vows of poverty, chastity and obedience. Our life includes daily participation in the Eucharist and the Divine Office, prayer, and ministry to those in need. We also have married or single Oblates, who commit themselves to a Rule of life and service in the Church, and Associates, who make up the wider family of CSJB.

We live by an Augustinian Rule, which emphasizes community spirit. Those who live with us include Oblates and friends, as well as our pony, dog, and cat. Our Retreat House and guest wing are often full of persons seeking spiritual direction and sacred space. Our buildings are set in a beautiful wooded area.

Our work includes spiritual direction, retreats, hospitality, and youth ministry. We work with young people in local parishes and at a rehabilitation center on our property. Each Sister is encouraged to develop her gifts, as a part of the whole calling of the Community. Our motto is: "He must increase, I must decrease." (John 3:30)

Lauds
7.30 am

Eucharist
8.00 am

Terce
9.30 am

Noonday Office
12 noon

Vespers
5.00 pm

Compline
8.30 pm

Office Book:
Our own book based upon the Book of Common Prayer of the Episcopal Church of the USA

SISTER BARBARA JEAN CSJB
(*Sister Superior, assumed office 2 October 1997*)
SISTER LAURA KATHARINE CSJB (*Assistant Superior*)

Sister Margaret Helena
Sister Suzanne Elizabeth
Sister Mary Lynne
Sister Deborah Frances
Sister Margo Elizabeth
Sister Mary Neale

Novices: 2

Community Publication
Michaelmas, Christmas & Easter Newsletters.

Community History & Books
James Simpson & Edward Story, *Stars in His Crown*, Ploughshare Press, Sea Bright, NJ, 1976
Valerie Bonham, *A Joyous Service*, CSJB, Windsor 1989;
Valerie Bonham,*A Place in Life*, CSJB, Windsor, 1992;
Valerie Bonham,*The Sisters of the Raj*, CSJB, Windsor,1997
P Allan, M Berry, D Hiley, Pamela CSJB & E Warrell, *An English Kyriale.*

Community Wares
Tote bags, mugs, cards, jewelry, candles, ornaments.

Guest and Retreat Facilities
ST MARGUERITE'S RETREAT HOUSE
This has twenty-five rooms. The address is the same as for the Convent but the telephone number is: *973 543 4582*
CONVENT GUEST WING
This has eight rooms (for women only).
The cost is $55.00 for an overnight stay with three meals. Closed Mondays.
Please telephone between 10 am and 5 pm.

Oblates & Associates
Oblates make promises which are renewed annually. The Rule of Life includes prayer, study, service, spiritual direction, retreats. Associates keep a simple Rule. Membership is ecumenical.

Community of St John the Divine

CSJD

Founded 1848

St John's House
652 Alum Rock Road
Birmingham
B8 3NS
UK
Tel: 0121 327 4174

Office Book:
Celebrating Common Prayer

Registered Charity:
No. MAR 210 254

Since the time of our foundation, we have always been a pioneering community. In the early years of our history, the Community played an important part in the establishing of new standards for Nursing and Midwifery, both in hospitals and in people's homes, as well as responding to health epidemics at home and abroad.

The Community has responded in more recent years to the challenge of change in Religious Life. The ethos of CSJD has broadened to cover all aspects of health, healing, reconciliation and pastoral care in its widest context ... ministries that all seek in helping people to find wholeness. The underpinning of our life and work is a spirituality based on St John, the Apostle of Love.

The exploration of the way ahead is based on much prayer, reflection and discussion. This is bringing to birth a new model for the Community. We now accept Lay members, who live with the Community for one year. This offers a structured life of prayer, work and study, which provides time and space for discernment of where God is leading each person. There is no expectation that Lay members will ask to enter the Novitiate, although this is one possibility, but it is broader in its aim. It is an encouragement for each member to explore their own spiritual journey and where the Lord is leading them.

We are still at the beginning of this new chapter. Yet, as the Community celebrated its 150th Anniversary in 1998, we pray we may be open and responsive to God's leading and that there will be others called to share the challenge and commitment of our future direction.

The corporate life of the Community centres around a weekday daily Eucharist celebrated in the House and the fourfold Office taken from *Celebrating Common Prayer*. On Sundays, Sisters attend local churches of their choice.

MOTHER CHRISTINE CSJD
(Revd Mother Superior, assumed office February 1992)
SISTER MARGARET ANGELA CSJD *(Assistant Superior)*

Sister Audrey	Sister Pamela
Sister Madeline	Sister Elaine
Sister Teresa	Sister Ivy
Sister Dorien	
Sister Marie-Clare	*Novices:* 1

Obituaries

1 Sep 1998 Sister Margaret Faith, aged 90, professed 51 years, Revd Mother Superior 1962-77

11 May 1999 Sister Monica, aged 74, professed 42 years

St John's House, Birmingham

Community Publication
Annual Report.

Community History
The brochure written for the 150th anniversary contains a short history.

Community Wares
Various hand-crafted cards for different occasions.

Guest and Retreat Facilities
Quiet Days for individuals and groups. Facilities for residential individual private retreats. We hope to develop a spirituality centre here in partnership with clergy and laity in the diocese.

Most convenient time to telephone: 9.00 am, 2.30 pm, 6.00 pm

Associates
Associates are men and women from all walks of life who desire to have a close link with the Community. They are formally admitted and wear a distinctive cross of the Community. They make a simple commitment to God ... to the Community ... and to each other, and together with the Community they form a network of prayer, fellowship and mutual support within Christ's ministry of wholeness and reconciliation. Those eligible to be Associates are confirmed members of the Anglican Church or full members of other recognised Christian churches.

Friends of the Community
Friends of the Community are people who request their names to be put on our mailing list. They maintain a link with the Community and undertake to pray regularly for the Community.

Community of St John the Evangelist

CSJE

Founded 1912

St Mary's Home
Pembroke Park
Ballsbridge
Dublin 4
IRISH REPUBLIC

Tel: 1 660 2904

Lauds
7.30 am
followed by Eucharist (when a priest is available)

Terce
8.50 am

Sext
12 noon

None
after lunch

Vespers
5.00 pm

Compline
8.00 pm

Office Book:
Hours of Prayer with the Revised Psalter

Founded in Dublin in 1912, CSJE was an attempt to establish Religious Life in the Church of Ireland, although it did not receive official recognition. The founder believed that a group of sisters living hidden lives of prayer and service would exercise a powerful influence. When he died in 1939, there were twenty-four professed sisters and six novices.

From the 1930s, the Community had a branch house in Wales, which became the Mother House in 1967. In 1996, however, the Sisters returned to Dublin to the house originally taken over in 1959 from the Community of St Mary the Virgin. (This CSMV was not connected with the CSMV sisters at Wantage, but was a small community founded in the 1890s which had never grown beyond nine members.) The present house was formerly a school and then a home for elderly ladies of the Church of Ireland. It is now a Registered Nursing and Residential Home under the care of the Community but run by lay people.

The remaining six Sisters of CSJE continue to live the Religious Life to the best of their ability and leave the future in the hands of God.

MOTHER CATHERINE MARGARET CSJE
(Mother Superior, assumed office January 1956)
Professed sisters: 6

Community History
A private booklet was produced for Associates in 1962.

Associates and Companions
Associates have a simple Rule, Companions a fuller and stricter Rule. Both groups are now much reduced in number.

St John, from the Book of Kells,
drawn by a sister CHC

Community of St Laurence

CSL

Founded 1874

Convent of St Laurence
Field Lane
Belper
Derby
DE56 1DD
UK

Tel: 01773 822585
&
01773 823390

Registered Charity:
No. 220282

The Community was founded in 1874. Its work was with the poor, not only the materially destitute, but also those in need of love and care. The sisters also cared for orphans. For over a hundred years, the Community was caring for ladies, who again needed love and care. They were known as Treasures, because the Community followed the life of St Laurence, our patron, whose Treasures were amongst the poor and needy. Owing to present-day circumstances, this work was gradually phased out. After much prayer and thought, we seemed to be guided to take up retreat work.

The Community has always been a small family, never at any time exceeding fourteen sisters. The Community is willing to accept women in their forties, who are seeking a life of prayer in an active community and desire to give themselves to God to test out their vocation in Religious Life.

MOTHER JEAN MARY CSL
(Mother Superior, assumed office 1995)
Professed Sisters: 6

Obituaries

7 Mar 1998	Sister Joyce Mary, aged 78, professed 48 years
23 Feb 1999	Sister Dorothy, aged 85, professed 42 years

Community Publication
Gridiron, which is free of charge.

Community Wares
Books, cards and preserves.

Guest and Retreat Facilities
Twenty-four single and seven twin-bedded rooms for men or women guests. The house is available for conferences and retreats, both individual or conducted, quiet days for groups or individual guests. Guidance is available from one of the sisters if required. The house is also open for visitors to spend Christmas or Easter with us. Hospitality is an important part of our life together with prayer.

Associates
Associates pray regularly for the community, and include priests and lay people. There are days organised at the Convent for the associates, at which new members may be admitted, and also retreats. We have over one hundred associates.

Community of St Mary (Eastern Province)

CSM

Founded 1865

St Mary's Convent
John Street
Peekskill
NY 10566-2130
USA

Tel: 914 737 0113
Fax: 914 737 4019
E-Mail:
compunun@aol.com

Matins
6.35 am
(7.35 am Sat & Sun)

Mass
7.00 am
(8.00 am Sat & Sun)

Terce
9.15 am

Sext
12 noon

Vespers
5.20 pm

Compline
8.05 pm

The Sisters of St Mary in Peekskill live a vowed life in community, centered around the daily Eucharist and a five-fold Divine Office. Each sister has time daily for private prayer and study. Our way of life is a modern expression of traditional monastic practice including silent meals in common, plainchant in English for much of our corporate worship, a distinctive habit, and a measure of enclosure.

Our ministry is an outward expression of our vowed life of poverty, chastity and obedience. the specific nature of our work has changed over the years since Mother Harriet and our first sisters were asked to take charge of the House of Mercy in New York City in 1865. Being "mindful of the needs of others," as our table blessing says, we have been led in many ways to care for the lost, forgotten and underprivileged. Today our work is primarily hospitality, retreats, pastoral counselling and exploration of outreach through the Internet. Sisters also go out from time to time to speak in parishes, lead quiet days and visit the sick in nursing homes. We serve on the Boards of St Mary's Hospital for Children and its affiliates.

MOTHER MIRIAM CSM
(*Mother Superior, assumed office 31 August 1996*)
SISTER MARY JEAN CSM (*Assistant Superior*)

Sister Anastasia	Sister Mary Francis
Sister Mary Basil	Sister Mary Angela
Sister Mary Helen	Sister Catherine Clare
Sister Mary Electa	Sister Mary Elizabeth

Community Publication
St Mary's Messenger. Contact the subscriptions editor. Cost to subscribers in the USA is $5, to those outside the USA $10.

Community History
Sister Mary Hilary CSM, *Ten Decades of Praise,* DeKoven Foundation, Racine, WI, 1965.
(*out of print*).

Community Wares
Assorted illuminated greeting cards.

Guest and Retreat Facilities
ST BENEDICT'S HOUSE is a modern building, containing eighteen single rooms and one apartment with twin beds. There is a dining room which can be converted into a chapel. A small book store and library are available for guests.

The Sisters of the Community of St Mary at Peekskill

ST GABRIEL'S HOUSE has a few rooms for guests, and a large multi-functional room for meetings or chapel services, with a small kitchenette for making coffee and tea. This room can seat up to fifty people comfortably. All meals at the Convent are in silence (except Sunday supper and major feast days). Dinner can be arranged at St Benedict's House on Friday night to accommodate groups arriving late.

Associates

Associates of the Community of St Mary are Christian men and women who undertake a Rule of life under the direction of the Community, and share in the support and fellowship of the Sisters, and of one another, whilst living dedicated and disciplined lives in the world. Any baptized, practising Christian who feels called to share in the life and prayer of the Community of St Mary as part of our extended family is welcome to inquire about becoming an Associate.

Each prospective Associate plans his or her own Rule with the advice of a Sister. An outline is provided covering one's share in the Eucharist and the Divine Office; a rule of private prayer; abstinence and fasting; and charity and witness. Individual vocations and circumstances vary so widely in today's world that a 'one size fits all' Rule is no longer appropriate. We do ask Associates to pray specifically for the Community, as we do for them, and, because the Divine Office is central to our way of life, to undertake some form of Daily Office. An Associate is also expected to keep in touch with us, and to seek to bring others to know the Community.

Office Book

The Monastic Diurnal Revised, (The Community of St Mary, New York, 1989): a modern English version of the *Monastic Diurnal* by Canon Winfred Douglas with supplemental texts based upon the American 1979 Book of Common Prayer. Copies are for sale.

Community of St Mary
(Western Province)

CSM

Founded 1865

Mary's Margin
S 83 W 27815 Beaver Trail
Mukwonago
WI 53149
USA

Tel & Fax: 414 363 8489
E-Mail:
srstmary@execpc.com

Meditation
7.30 am

Morning Prayer
8.00 am

Walking the Labyrinth Meditation
Once a day

Evening Prayer
5.00 pm

Compline
9.00 pm

Office Book:
Book of Common Prayer of the Episcopal Church of the USA

Founded in 1865 in New York City, the Community of St Mary is the oldest indigenous Religious Order in the Episcopal Church. The Sisters are dedicated to any form of service of which a woman is capable, inspired, and informed by a life of prayer. The Community today consists of three independent Provinces, each guided by a common Rule.

The Sisters of St Mary first came to Wisconsin in 1878 to assume management of Kemper Hall, a boarding school in Kenosha. Over the years, they have also run St Mary's Home in Chicago, the DeKoven Center and St Mary's Camp in Racine, a parish day school in California and a retreat house in Colorado.

Today, there are seven Sisters in the Western Province, who live singly or in small groups, devoting themselves to prayer and service according to their gifts and sense of God's guidance. They gather regularly to conduct business and celebrate fellowship with one another.

In July 1993, the Sisters purchased Mary's Margin, to be a house of prayer where they could offer hospitality to individuals for private retreats and to small day groups for meetings and quiet days. Nestled in wooded hills overlooking the Fox River Valley, it provides an exceptionally beautiful and peaceful 'breathing space'. A unique labyrinth has recently been completed, using the winding paths through the five acres of woods, ending in a sixteen-foot tower overlooking the Vernon Wildlife Marsh.

SISTER LETITIA PRENTICE CSM
(*Sister superior, assumed office January 1992*)
SISTER MARY GRACE ROM CSM (*Assistant superior*)
Sister Mary Faith Burgess
Sister Jean Hodgkins
Sister Mary Paula Bush
Sister Dorcas Baker
Sister Sarah Anne Ilsley

Obituaries

22 Feb 1997 — Sister Mary Stephen Gilkerson, aged 65, professed 44 years
27 May 1999 — Sister Virginia Smith, aged 81, professed 51 years

Community Publication

St Mary's Messenger and *Margin Notes*.
They are sent out three or four times a year. There is no charge. Write to the community address.

Community History

Sister Mary Hilary CSM, *Ten Decades of Praise,* DeKoven Foundation, Racine, WI, 1965.

Guest and Retreat Facilities

There are two guest rooms for overnight - for men or women guests. There is a $25 deposit with every booking, which can be refunded on arrival or else designated as a donation. There is room for up to twelve people for day workshops or quiet days.

Sister Dorcas is available to lead dance workshops (sacred or recreational) for parishes, conferences, or special events.

Vigil-Eucharists are held most Saturdays beginning at 4pm. These include instruction and practice in dance, music and meditation and are open to anyone interested. After the Eucharist, all are invited to a simple vegetarian supper. Directed retreats for up to eight people are also offered or may be arranged. For further information, contact Sister Dorcas at Mary's Margin.

Oblates and Associates

Oblates and Associates are part of the community family and they follow a Rule of Life and assist the sisters as they are able.

Community of St Mary the Virgin

CSMV

Founded 1848

St Mary's Convent
Challow Road
Wantage
Oxfordshire
OX12 9DJ
UK

Tel: 01235 763141

01235 760170
(Guest Wing)

The Community of St Mary the Virgin was founded in 1848 by William John Butler, then Vicar of Wantage. As Sisters, we are called to respond to our vocation in the spirit of the Blessed Virgin Mary: "Behold, I am the handmaid of the Lord. Let it be to me according to your word." Our common life is centred in the worship of God through the Eucharist, the daily Office and in personal prayer. From this all else flows. For some it will be expressed in outgoing ministry in neighbourhood and parish, or in living alongside those in inner city areas. For others, it will be expressed in spiritual direction, preaching and retreat giving, in creative work in studio and press, or in forms of healing ministry. Sisters also live and work among the elderly at St Katharine's House, our dual-registered Home for Elderly People in Wantage. The Community has been in India and South Africa for many years and has involvement in the nurturing and training of a small indigenous community in Madagascar (see entry for the FMJK).

MOTHER BARBARA CLAIRE CSMV
(Revd Mother, assumed office 8 December 1997)

The Community numbers eighty-nine Sisters and has a Novitiate which normally numbers about six.

Obituaries
Sisters Mary Mechtild, Elizabeth Mary, Francis Hilda, Rhona, Marjorie Michael, Kathleen Mary, Bertha Mary, Sylvia, Elizabeth, Ella Mary and Frances Mary have died.

Other Addresses

St Peter's Bourne
40 Oakleigh Park South
London N20 9JN
UK
Tel: 0208 445 5535

366 High Street
Smethwick
B66 3PD
UK
Tel: 0121 558 0094

St Katharine's House
Ormond Road
Wantage
Oxfordshire OX12 8EA
UK
Tel: 01235 762739

St Mary's Lodge
Challow Road
Wantage
Oxfordshire OX12 9DH
UK
Tel: 01235 767112

Christa Prema
Seva Sangha
Shivajinagar
Pune 411005
Maharastra
INDIA

3 Keurboom Avenue
Omega Park
Brakpan 1541
SOUTH AFRICA

Community History
A Hundred Years of Blessing, SPCK, London, 1946.

Community Wares
The Printing Press offers a variety of cards. Catalogues are available from the Sister in charge of the Press at St Mary's Convent.

Guest and Retreat Facilities

ST MARY'S CONVENT The Sisters welcome to the Guest Wing those who wish to spend time in rest, retreat and silence within the setting of a Religious Community. Our particular emphasis is on hospitality to individuals, and where requested we try to arrange individual guidance with a Sister. We are also able to accommodate a small number of groups for retreats and Quiet Days.

ST PETER'S BOURNE This is a retreat house especially suitable for individual guests or small groups. Resident guests have the use of a large sitting room overlooking the garden, as well as Chapel and library. Day groups are accommodated separately in the 'Coachhouse' where the facilities are self-catering. All guests are welcome to join in the daily Eucharist.

Most convenient time to telephone: 8.15 am - 12.15 pm, 5.30 pm - 6.30 pm

Oblates
The Oblates of the Community respond to their vocation in the same spirit as Mary: "Behold, I am the handmaid of the Lord. Let it be to me according to your word." Oblates may be married or single, women or men, ordained or lay. The majority are Anglicans, but members of other denominations are also accepted. There is a common Rule, based on Scripture and the Rule of St Augustine, and each Oblate also draws up a personal Rule of Life in consultation with the Oblates' Sister. There is a two-year period of testing as an Oblate Novice; the Promise made at full Oblation is renewed annually. In addition to their close personal link with the Community, Oblates meet in regional groups and support each other in prayer and fellowship.

Associates
Associates are men and women, ordained and lay, who wish to be united in prayer and fellowship with the Community, sharing in the spirit of Mary's 'Fiat' in their daily lives. Each Associate has a Rule of Life and is expected to keep in touch with the Associates' Sister, by letter or by visiting. Daily prayer for the Community is undertaken. The Community keeps in touch with the Associates through a monthly newsletter, and each year an Associates' Day is held at the Convent. All Associates are required to make an annual retreat. There are about two hundred and fifty Associates worldwide, and another fifty in the South African Province who have their own Associates' Sister and monthly newsletter but who also receive the English Monthly Letter.

Community of St Michael & All Angels

CSM&AA

Founded 1874

St Michael's House
PO Box 79
9300 Bloemfontein
SOUTH AFRICA

Tel: 051 522 0440
Tel: 051 522 6546

Residential:
St Michael's House
52 De Bruyn Street
Universitas
Bloemfontein
SOUTH AFRICA

Mass is celebrated most days and a modified Office timetable is used.

Officc Book:
1989 Anglican Prayer Book of the Church of the Province of Southern Africa

The Community of St Michael and All Angels was founded by the second Bishop of Bloemfontein, Allan Becher Webb, for pioneer work in his vast diocese, which included the Orange Free State, Basutoland, Griqualand West and into the Transvaal. The sisters were active in mission, nursing and education. Sister Henrietta Stockdale became the founder of professional nursing in South Africa. In 1874, other sisters established St Michael's School for Girls in Bloemfontein, which still exists today as one of the leading schools in South Africa.

Today, the sisters are only four in number, perhaps indicating that their work is nearly done. It would seem that the call has been answered.

SISTER DOREEN MARY BALL CSM&AA
(*Revd Mother, assumed office 30 November 1987*)
Sister Mary Ruth Brewster
Sister Joan Marsh
Sister Thirza Dorey

Obituaries

1 Apr 1997	Sister Constance Sparrow, aged 88, professed 41 years
21 Jun 1997	Sister Marion Faith Bucklow, aged 101, professed 54 years

Community History

Margaret Leith, *One the Faith,* 1971
Mary Brewster, *One the Earnest Looking Forward,* 1991
Obtainable from St Michael's School, PO Box 12110, Brandhof 9324, SOUTH AFRICA

Community Wares

Cards etc.

Guest and Retreat Facilities

St Michael's House has a self-contained guest flat, with service, available for men or women guests.

Associates

The Associates of CSM&AA in South Africa meet four or five times a year at St Michael's House. They keep a simple Rule and have an annual residential retreat in the country at a Roman Catholic religious house and farm in the Eastern Free State. There are a few Associates in England.

Community of St Peter

CSP

Founded 1861

St Peter's Convent
Maybury Hill
Woking
Surrey
GU22 8AE
UK

Tel: 01483 761137
Fax: 01483 714775

Lauds
7.00 am

Terce
9.15 am

Sext
12.45 pm
(12.50 pm Sun)

Vespers
5.00 pm

Compline
8.00 pm

Mass
7.30 am (10 am Tue & Fri; Sung 10 am Sun)

Office Book:
CSMV Office

Registered Charity:
No. 240675

The Sisters have registered homes (nursing/care) for elderly women and women in need of a protected environment. St Columba's Retreat House is under their care and they also have close links with the Society of the Holy Cross in Korea, a Sisterhood founded by St Peter's Community (see separate entry, page 126).

The Eucharist is celebrated daily at the Convent and the Sisters are committed to a fivefold daily Office.

REVD MOTHER MARGARET PAUL CSP
(Mother Superior, assumed office 1973)
SISTER GEORGINA RUTH CSP *(Assistant Superior)*

Sister Hilary	Sister Angela
Sister Dorothy	Sister Teresa Mary
Sister Constance Margaret	Sister Joyce
Sister Margery Grace	Sister Rosamund
Sister Joy	Sister Lucy Clare
Sister Jane Margery	Sister Caroline Jane

Community Publication
Associates' leaflet at Christmas and Pentecost.

Community History
Elizabeth Cuthbert, *In St Peter's Shadow*, CSP, Woking, 1994.

Community Wares
Cards.

St Peter's Convent, Woking

St Columba's House (Retreat and Conference Centre)

Guest and Retreat Facilities

ST COLUMBA'S HOUSE *Director:* Paul Jenkins
St Columba's House (Retreat & Conference Centre)
Maybury Hill, Woking, Surrey GU22 8AE, UK
Tel: 01483 766498 Fax: 01483 740441
E-Mail: retreats@st. columba.org.uk

Twenty-five bedrooms, disabled suite, self-catering flat, etc. A programme of individual and group retreats.
Also a conference centre for residential and day use. Refurbished in 1998 to an exceptionally high standard for retreatants, parish groups, and day / overnight consultations. An outstanding liturgical space with a pastoral, and liturgical programme. A place to retreat and reflect on life's journey.

Most convenient time to telephone: 8.00 am - 5.00 pm.

Associates

The associates' fellowship meets twice a year at Petertide and Christmas. The associates support the community in prayer and with practical help, as they are able. They have a simple rule, sharing a daily Office and attending the Eucharist as their individual commitments permit.

Community of St Peter, Horbury

CSPH

Founded 1858

St Peter's Convent
Dovecote Lane
Horbury
Wakefield
West Yorkshire
WF4 6BB
UK

Tel: 01924 272181
Fax: 01924 261225

Lauds
6.30 am

Mass
7.30 am

Midday Office
12.00 noon

Vespers
6.00 pm

Compline
9.00 pm

The Community seeks to glorify God by a life of loving dedication to him, by worship and by serving him in others. A variety of pastoral work is undertaken including retreat and mission work, social work and ministry to individuals in need. The spirit of the community is Benedictine and the recitation of the Divine Office central to the life.

MOTHER ROBINA CSPH
(Revd Mother, assumed office 14 Apr 1993)
SISTER ELIZABETH CSPH *(Assistant Superior)*

Sister Gwynneth Mary	Sister Phyllis
Sister Margaret	Sister Jean Clare
Sister Mary Clare *(priest)*	Sister Monica

Sister Margaret Ann,
2 Main Street, Bossall, York YO2 7NT, UK
Tel: 01904 468253

Obituaries
3 Jan 1999 Sister Veronica, aged 87, professed 60 years

Community Publication
Annual Review.

Guest and Retreat Facilities
A separate guest wing has four single rooms, with shower room and utility room.

Oblates and Associates
The Community has both oblates and associates.

The Chapel of the Community of St Peter, Horbury

Community of the Servants of the Cross

CSC

Founded 1877

Marriott House
Tollhouse Close
Chichester
PO19 3EZ
UK
Tel: 01243 781620

The Community has an Augustinian Rule and for much of their history the sisters have cared for elderly and infirm women. In 1997, the Sisters left their convent at Lindfield in Sussex and some moved to Marriott House, a retirement home in Chichester, and others to the Community of St Peter at Woking. They are now known as:

MOTHER ANGELA AND THE HOLY ROOD SISTERS.

They use a local church for Mass and the Offices.

MOTHER ANGELA CSC (*Mother Superior*)

8 *Professed sisters*

****

CSWG; graphics: Viccari Wheele, Brighton

The blessing at Lauds at the CSWG monastery at Hove
(see next page)

Community of the Servants of the Will of God

CSWG

Founded 1953

The Monastery of the Holy Trinity
Crawley Down
Crawley
West Sussex
RH10 4LH
UK
Tel: 01342 712074

The Monastery of Christ the Saviour
23 Cambridge Road
Hove
East Sussex BN3 1DE, UK
Tel: 01273 726698

Vigils 5.00 am
Lauds 7.00 am
Terce 9.30 am
Sext 12.00 noon
None 1.45 pm
Vespers 6.30 pm

Mass
7.00 pm Mon - Fri
11.00 am Sat & Sun

Office Book:
CSWG Divine Office and Chant

This monastery is set in woodland with a small farm attached. The Community lives a contemplative life, uniting silence, work and prayer in a simple life style based on the Rule of St Benedict. The Community is especially concerned with uniting the traditions of East and West, and has developed the Liturgy, Divine Office and use of the Jesus Prayer accordingly. The Community has another monastery at Hove, living under the same Rule, so as to bring Christ into this Urban Priority Area through the life of prayer. Both monasteries now include women living under the same monastic Rule.

FATHER GREGORY CSWG
(Father Superior, assumed office 14 September 1973)
FATHER BRIAN CSWG *(Prior, at Hove)*

CRAWLEY DOWN
Father Gregory *(Superior)*
Father Colin *(Prior)*
Father Peter
Brother John Baptist
Brother John of the Cross
Brother Andrew
Sister Mary Ruth
Brother Seraphim
Brother Cuthbert
Novices: 2

HOVE
Father Brian *(Prior)*
Brother Mark
Brother Martin
Sister Mary Angela
Brother Steven
Brother Christopher Mark

Community Publication
CSWG *Newsletter*, issued Advent & Pentecost. Write to the Monastery of the Holy Trinity.

Guest and Retreat Facilities
CRAWLEY DOWN: six individual guest rooms; meals in community refectory; Divine Office and Eucharist, all with modal chant.

HOVE: two individual guest rooms; other facilities comparable to Crawley Down.

Most convenient time to telephone: 9.30 am - 6.00 pm.

Community Wares
Mounted icon prints, Jesus Prayer ropes, candles and vigil lights, booklets on monastic and spiritual life.

Associates
The associates keep a rule of life in the spirit of the monasteries.

Community of the Sisters of the Church

CSC

Founded 1870

for the whole people of God

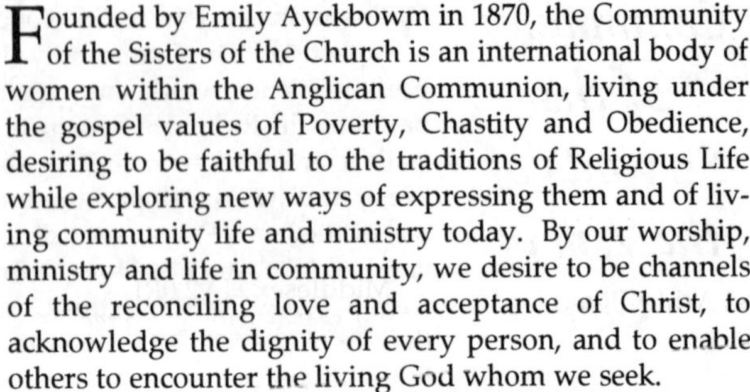

Founded by Emily Ayckbowm in 1870, the Community of the Sisters of the Church is an international body of women within the Anglican Communion, living under the gospel values of Poverty, Chastity and Obedience, desiring to be faithful to the traditions of Religious Life while exploring new ways of expressing them and of living community life and ministry today. By our worship, ministry and life in community, we desire to be channels of the reconciling love and acceptance of Christ, to acknowledge the dignity of every person, and to enable others to encounter the living God whom we seek.

The Community's patrons are St Michael and the angels pointing us to a life both of worship and active ministry, of mingled adoration and action.

Our name, Sisters of the Church, reminds us that our particular dedication is to the mystery of the Church as the Body of Christ in the world.

The houses have varying timetables of corporate worship. The Eucharist and Divine Office (usually fourfold) are the heart of our Community life.

SISTER ANITA CSC
(Mother Superior & English Provincial, assumed office 1 March 1998)

ENGLAND

SISTER VALERIE CSC
(Assistant English Provincial)

Aileen
Annaliese
Ann Mechtilde
Beryl
Catherine
Dorothea
Gillian
Hilda Mary
Jennifer
Judith
Kim Marie
Lydia
Lynn
Marietta
Marguerite Mae
Mary Josephine
Patricia
Robin Elizabeth
Rosina
Ruth
Sheila Julian
Susan
Vivien
Novices: 1

Registered Charity No. for CSC: 271790

Registered Charity No. for CEA: 200240

Obituaries

2 Nov 1998	Sister Joy, aged 92, professed 62 years
25 Feb 1999	Sister Bernadette, aged 95, professed 69 years

St Michael's Convent
56 Ham Common
Richmond
Surrey TW10 7JH
Tel: 0208 940 8711
& 0208 948 2502
Fax: 0208 332 2927

82 Ashley Road
Bristol BS6 5NT
Tel: 01179 413268
Fax: 01179 086620

St Gabriel's
27A Dial Road
Clevedon
North Somerset BS21 7HL
Tel: 01275 872586

10 Furness Road
West Harrow
Middlesex HA2 0RL
Tel & Fax: 0208 423 3780

112 St Andrew's Road
North
St Anne's-on-Sea
Lancashire FY8 2JQ
Tel: 01253 728016

CANADA

SISTER MICHAEL CSC
(*Provincial, assumed office December 1997*)

Elsa
Heather
Margaret
Mary Adela
Rita

St Michael's House
127 Burgundy Road
Oakville
Ontario L6J 6R1
Tel: 905 844 9511 *Fax: 905 842 6529*
E-Mail: csc@tap.net
Website: http://www.tap.net/csc

19 Cardinal Mindszenty Boulevard
St Elizabeth Village
Hamilton
Ontario L9B 2M3
Tel & Fax: 905 387 5659

AUSTRALIA

SISTER HELEN CSC
(*Provincial, assumed office October 1996*)

Audrey
Elisa Helen
Elspeth
Elizabeth May

Fiona
Frances
Linda Mary
Marina

Marguerite
Rosamund
Scholastica

216 Mahoney's Road
East Burwood
Victoria 3151
Tel: 3 9802 1955
Fax: 3 9802 6642

96 Hertford Street
Glebe
NSW 2037
Tel: 2 660 5708
Fax: 2 9692 0173

The House of Prayer
42 Wirrang Drive
Dondingalong
Via Kempsey
NSW 2440
Tel: 2 65 669 244
Fax: 2 65 669 165

44/1 St Kilda Road
St Kilda
Victoria 3182
Tel & Fax: 3 9593 9590

SOLOMON ISLANDS

SISTER PHYLLIS CSC
(*Sister Co-ordinator, assumed office October 1998*)

Annie
Carrie
Christina
Doreen
Jennifer Betty
Joanna
Kate
Kathleen

Lilian
Louisa
Lucy
Martha
May
Mercy
Miriam
Muriel

Rebecca
Ruth Anne
Sarah Palmer
Veronica

Novices: 13
Postulants: 5

PO Box A7
Auki
Malaita

Patteson House
Box 50
Honiara
Tel: 22413
Fax: 21098

Tetete ni Kolivuti
Box 510
Honiara

St Mary's
Luesala
Diocese of Temotu
Santa Cruz

St Gabriel's
c/o Hanuato'o Diocese
Kira Kira
Makira/Ulawa Province
Fax: 50128

Addresses of Affiliated Communities

Society of Our Lady St Mary
Bethany Place
PO Box 762
Digby
Nova Scotia BOV 1AO
CANADA

Community of the Love of God
(*Orthodox Syrian*)
Nazareth
Kadampanad South 691553
Pathanamthitta District
Kerala
INDIA

Community Publication
Newsletter, three times a year, the editor of which is Sister Audrey in Australia (St Kilda address). However, information can be obtained from any house of the community.

Community History
A Valiant Victorian: The Life and Times of Mother Emily Ayckbowm 1836-1900 of the Community of the Sisters of the Church, Mowbray, London, 1964.

Community Wares
These vary from house to house, but some sell crafts and cards. Vestments are made in the Solomon Islands.

Guest and Retreat Facilities
Hospitality is offered in most houses. Where it is the main ministry, the accommodation, facilities and programmes are appointed and shaped to this end. Facilities vary from house to house and so contact should be made with a particular house for specific details.

Associates
Associates are men and women who seek to live the Gospel values of Simplicity, Chastity and Obedience within their own circumstances. Each creates his/her own Rule of Life and has a Link Sister or Link House. They are united in spirit with CSC in its life of worship and service, fostering a mutually enriching bond.

Office Book used by the Community
The Office varies in the different Provinces. Various combinations of the Community's own Office book, the New Zealand psalter and the most recent prayer books of Australia, Canada and Melanesia.

Community of the Sisters of the Love of God

SLG

Founded 1906

Convent of the Incarnation
Fairacres
Oxford OX4 1TB
UK
Tel: 01865 721301
Fax: 01865 250798

Matins 2.00 am

Lauds 6.10 am (6.40 am Sun)

Terce & Mass 9.05 am

Sext 12.15 pm

None 2.05 pm (3.00 pm Sun)

Vespers 6.00 pm (5.30 pm Sun)

Compline 8.35 pm (8.05 pm Sun)

Office Book: SLG Office

Registered Charity: No. 261722; SLG Charitable Trust Ltd: registered in England 990049

A contemplative community whose chief work is prayer built on the offering of the Eucharist (daily at the Mother House) and the regular recitation of the Divine Office by day and night. Life and prayer in solitude is recognised as an important part of the Sisters' vocation, in accordance with the Carmelite spirit of the community.

MOTHER ROSEMARY SLG
(Revd Mother, assumed office 1996)

Sister Margaret Clare
Sister Mary Angela
Sister Josephine
Sister Mary Magdalene
Sister Mary Augustine
Sister Mary Margaret
Sister Benedicta
Sister Isabel Mary
Sister Mary Joseph
Sister Adrian
Sister Edna Monica
Sister Anne
Sister Jane Frances
Sister Mary Kathleen
Sister Edwina
Sister Julia
Sister Esther Mary
Sister Barbara June
Sister Susan
Sister Edmée
Sister Teresa
Sister Ellinor
Sister Christine
Sister Cynthia
Sister Helen Columba
Sister Catherine
Sister Patricia Thomas
Sister Sarah
Sister Julie
Sister Shirley Clare
Sister Avis Mary
Sister Alison Kathleen
Sister Tessa
Sister Margaret Theresa
Sister Raphael
Sister Raine
Sister Noel
Sister Barbara
Sister Stephanie Thérèse
Sister Clare
Sister Freda
Sister Judith
Sister Nicola

Novices: 6 *Postulants:* 2

Obituaries

23 Mar 1998	Sister Margaret, aged 76, professed 31 years
25 Dec 1998	Sister Helen Mary, aged 87, professed 47 years
6 Jul 1999	Sister Eileen Mary, aged 78, professed 43 years

Community Publication

Fairacres Chronicle.
Write to the Sister in charge, SLG Press, Convent of the Incarnation, Fairacres, Oxford OX4 1TB, UK, or fax *01865 790860.*

Community Wares

SLG Press publishes books and pamphlets on spirituality. A list of titles is available from the above address.

Convent of the Incarnation, Fairacres, Oxford

Addresses of other houses

Bede House, Goudhurst Road, Staplehurst, Tonbridge, Kent TN12 0HQ, UK
Tel: 01580 891262 Fax: 01580 890171

Convent of St Mary & the Angels, Woodland Avenue, Hemel Hempstead, Hertfordshire HP1 1RG, UK *Tel: 01442 256989 Fax: 01442 217009*

St Isaac's Retreat, PO Box 93, Opononi, Northland, AOTEOROA/NEW ZEALAND *Tel & Fax: 9 4058 834*

Guest and Retreat Facilities

There is limited accommodation for private retreats, for both men and women, at all houses of the Community. Please write to the Sister in Charge (or the Guest sister at Fairacres) to make a booking.

Most convenient time to telephone:

10.15 am - 11.45 am; 2.15 pm - 4.15 pm; 6.30 pm - 7.30 pm

Oblates and associates

The Community includes Oblate Sisters, who are called to the contemplative life in the world rather than within the monastic enclosure.

There are several other groups of associates: Priest Associates, Companions, and the Fellowship of the Love of God. Information about all these may be obtained from the Revd Mother at Fairacres.

Community of the Sisters of Melanesia

CSM

Founded 1980

KNT/Veranaaso
PO Box 19 (Church of Melanesia)
Honiara
SOLOMON ISLANDS

Mattins & Mass
5.45 am

Morning Office
7.45 am

Mid-day Office & Intercession
11.55 am

Afternoon Office
1.30 pm

Evensong & Meditation
5.30 pm

Compline
8.45 pm

Office Book:
CSM Office Book (adapted from the Office Book of the Melanesian Brotherhood)

Members of the Melanesian Brotherhood first suggested forming a Community of women in the 1960s, an idea which emerged from the mission experience, particularly their work with women and children. The Community of the Sisters of Melanesia finally came into being on 17 November 1980 when the first four women took vows of Obedience, Celibacy and Poverty. Nestar Atkin was the sister who had the vision, helped by Mary, Margaret, and Lilly.

SISTER CATHERINE ROSSER CSM
(*Head Sister, assumed office 12 May 1997*)
SISTER HELLEN KAHIHIRI CSM (*Assistant Head Sister*)

Sister Hilda Leta
Sister Dorothy Emi
Sister Salome Bulemelu
Sister Babra Sigihi
Sister Joan Mary Haeta
Sister Kate Toro
Sister Veronica Buloka
Sister Lealyn Inu
Sister Mary Dorah
Sister Veronica Haaliu
Sister Roselyn Kiko
Sister Georgina Ileo
Sister Nestar Rose
Sister Georgina Vagi
Sister Pauline Filei
Sister Janet Bechana
Sister Margaret Honiola
Sister Annica Sawa
Sister Webstar Mane
Sister Elsey Gaotee
Sister Hellen Matahia
Sister Ellen Gauba
Sister Lydia Dora
Sister Naery Fano
Sister Janet Keu
Sister Rebecca Kapupuni
Sister Grace Delight
Sister Jessica
Sister Esther Sau
Sister Rose Ella Rairamo
Sister Pamela Kotini
Sister Joylyn Dora
Sister Eily Muna
Sister Sussy Pituvaki
Sister Patricia
Sister Alice Alaki
Sister Sandra Teria
Sister Annie Boruboru
Sister Rose Tohe
Sister Rossar Kukulu
Sister Clera Deonadi
Sister Christina Norman
Sister Lillian Umatete
Sister Norah Jilly
Sister Regina Nunu
Sister Jessy Kolo
Sister Mavis Noli
Sister Laystone Esmy
Sister Hellen Fox
Sister Louisa Bako
Sister Pricilla
Sister Phylistus Qwai
Sister Phylistus Autedi

Novices: 21

Addresses of other houses

Joe Wate Household, Longa Bay, Waihi Parosh, Southern Region, SOLOMON ISLANDS
Wairokai Missionary Working Household, Wairokai Village, West Areare, Arekwa Region, SOLOMON ISLANDS
Nat Household, Bokoniseu.Vutu, Ghaobata Parish, East Honiara, SOLOMON ISLANDS

Community Wares
Vestments, altar linen, weaving and crafts.

Associates
The supporters of the Community of the Sisters of Melanesia are called Associates, a group established in 1990. It is an organisation for men and women, young and old, and has over one thousand members, including many young boys and girls. All promise to support the Sisters in prayer, and they are a great support in this and other ways.

Community of the Transfiguration

CT

Founded 1898

495 Albion Avenue
Cincinnati
Ohio 45246
USA

Tel: 513 771 5291
Fax: 513 771 0839

The Community of the Transfiguration, founded in 1898 by Eva Lee Matthews, is a Religious community of women dedicated to the mystery of the Transfiguration. Our life is one of prayer and service, reflecting the spirit of Mary and Martha, shown forth in spiritual, educational and social ministries. The Mother House of the community is located in Cincinnati, Ohio, where our ministries include hospitality, a school, a retirement/nursing home and a recreation center. The community also offers a retreat ministry on the West Coast; and in the Dominican Republic, the Sisters minister to malnourished children and their families through medical clinics and a pre-school.

The Sisters live their life under the vows of poverty, chastity and obedience. The motto of the community is Benignitas, Simplicitas and Hilaritas - Kindness, Simplicity and Joy.

Lauds, Morning Prayer
6.30 am

Holy Eucharist
7.00 am

Noon Office
12.30 pm

Evening Prayer
5.00 pm

Compline
8.15 pm

Other addresses

St Mary's Memorial Home, 469 Albion Avenue, Cincinnati, Ohio 45246, USA

Bethany School, 495 Albion Avenue, Glendale, Ohio 45246, USA

Sisters of the Transfiguration, 1633 "D" Street, Eureka, California 95501, USA

St Monica's Center, 10022 Chester Road, Cincinnati, Ohio 45215, USA

Sisters of theTranfiguration, EPS#G-2516, PO Box 02-5540, Miami, Florida 33102-5540, USA

Congregation of the Sisters of the Visitation of Our Lady

CVL

Founded 1964

Convent of the Visitation
Hetune
Box 18
Popondetta
Oro Province
Papua New Guinea

In the early 1960s, three young women accompanied a Holy Name Sister to Hetune, a site near Popondetta in the then Northern Province, in order to test their vocation to the Religious Life. The group became known as the Community of the Visitation and for the next twenty years remained concentrated at Hetune, making two attempts at opening further communities, first at Madang, then at Dotura.

The Congregation, on the basis of its spirituality springing from the life and discipleship of Our Lady, focuses its apostolate on the family which it undertakes through complementary ministries of hospitality within its own community houses and visiting in family homes and centres of family activity.

Sister Ann CVL *(Guardian)*
Sister Beverley CVL (*Coordinator, Hetune Convent*)
Sister Briget CVL (*Coordinator, Novice Formation*)
Sister Naomi Faith CVL
(*Coordinator, Goroka Community House*)
Professed Sisters: 11

Other House
House of Our Lady of Reconciliation, Box 1547, Goroka 441, Eastern Highlands Province, Papua New Guinea
Tel: 732 3190 *Fax (Church): 732 1214*

****

The Chapel at Ewell Monastery (see next page)

Ewell Monastery

Founded 1966

Ewell Monastery
Water Lane
West Malling
Kent
ME19 6HH
UK
FAX: 01732 870279

E-Mail: ewell@clara.co.uk

Website:
http://home.clara.net/ewell
&
http://www.ewell.clara.net/tomato/index.html

Vigils
4.30 am

Eucharist
7.30 am

Terce
8.25 am

Sext
12 noon

None
1.55 pm

Vespers
5.45 pm

Compline
7.45 pm

Office Book:
Ewell Vigils &
Ewell Monastic Day Hours

Ewell Monastery is an Anglican Cistercian monastery. Here the integrated monastic life of the Cistercian reform is followed by monks and lay people. Worship and prayer, work and study are lived out as a response to Christ. It is a commitment of Christian discipleship lived out in the communion of brothers in the solitude of the monastery. The monastery is situated on a six-acre site close to the village and yet secluded and quiet. We have an ecumenical spiritual affiliation with the Roman Catholic Cistercian Order.

FATHER AELRED ARNESEN
(Abba, elected 23 September 1978)

Brother Timothy Pritchard

Community Publication
Ewell Cistercians: broadsheet, published on 1 November each year.

Community Wares
CD-Rom: containing slide show of 220 photographs, the Ewell Website and Windows 6.00.002 Media Player and update Browsers. Cost: £4.75 including p & p.
Postcards of original photographs of Ewell Monastery: 25p each excluding p & p.

Guest and Retreat Facilities
There is a small guest house for visitors. Please write to make a reservation, giving alternative dates.

Associates
Ewell Cistercians (incorporating Friends and lay people of varying degrees of participation in the community).

Fileambanan my Mpano-mpovavin l Jesoa Kristy

(Society of the Servants of Jesus Christ)

FMJK

Founded 1985

Convent Hasina
BP 28
Ambohidratrimo 105
Antananarivo 101
MADAGASCAR

The FMJK sisters were founded by Canon Hall Speers in 1985. They live in the village of Tsinjohasina, on the high plateaux above the rice fields, situated some fifteen kilometres from Antananarivo, the capital of Madagascar. The sisters work in the village dispensary and are active in visiting, Christian teaching and pastoral work in the villages around. They are an independent community but have been nurtured by a connection with the Community of St Mary the Virgin, Wantage, in the UK.

SISTER GEORGETTE FMJK
(*sister-in-charge*)
Sister Ernestine
Sister Jeanne
Sister Jacqueline
Sister Isabelle
Sister Odette
Sister Sabine

Novices: 2

The FMJK Sisters

Korean Franciscan Brotherhood

KFB

Founded 1994

17-3 Chon Dong
Chung Gu
Inchon 400-190
Republic of Korea
Tel: 32 7720904
Fax: 32 7614047
E-Mail: kfb93@ netsgo.com

Web site: http:// www.freeyellow.com/ members4/kfb

Morning Prayer, Mass & Meditation
6.00 am

Midday Prayer
12 noon

Evening Prayer
5.30 pm

Night Prayer & Meditation
9.30 pm

Office Book:
The Daily Office SSF (in Korean translation)

The Korean Franciscan Brotherhood is a community in formation in the Anglican Church of Korea. It is supported by the Society of St Francis through the loan of one of their brothers as a mentor and through the visits of SSF Ministers, although KFB is not a part of SSF. The Brotherhood has also been greatly supported by the sisters of the Society of the Holy Cross in Seoul. The aims of the KFB are to contribute to the building up of God's kingdom by a life of witness through prayer and service. Its members take part in youth and spirituality programmes and assist with some local social welfare programmes. An important aspect is also that of promoting the idea of Religious community life as a possible vocation for young people.

Brother Christopher John SSF
(Mentor brother, on loan from the ANZ Province of SSF)

Novices: 2

Community Publication
The quarterly community newsletter is available in printed form (donation appreciated) or at the Web site.

Guest and Retreat Facilities
The community has two guest rooms available. As well as regular retreatants, visitors from overseas are welcome, or those making stopovers in Korea. The Brotherhood is situated about ninety minutes by bus or subway from the Kimpo International Airport in Seoul. If possible, overseas visitors can be met at the airport. Accommodation is by donation.

Brother Christopher John SSF with the KFB novices

Little Brothers of Francis

LBF

Founded 1987

"Eremophilia"
PO Box 162
Tabulam
NSW 2469
AUSTRALIA

Meditation
6.00 am

Morning Prayer
7.00 am

Compline
8.00 pm

Other Offices and times of prayer are said in the Hermitages.

Office Book:
Anglican Prayer Book of Australia & LBF Office

A deep longing for God is central to our way of life, and in Christ we see the perfect expression of God's longing and love for us. The Christ of the Gospels thus becomes the pattern of our lives. This same pattern was the inspiration of Francis's life.

It is the Francis whose life was Christ-centred; who sought places of solitude; who loved the whole of creation; and who tried to live a simple, uncluttered life,that has encouraged us in our Christian vocation. Accordingly LBF have chosen to live outside a small country town in the rocky foothills of the mountains, locally described as 'rubbish country'. There we try to touch the primitive spirit that moulded the beginning of the Franciscan family, especially the tradition of the hermitages.

The lifestyle of the brothers is reflected in the way the property is set out, with individual huts scattered through the bush around a central community building. The huts provide each brother with a place of solitude, while the community area is for times of communal work, worship, meals, etc. We try to be as self-supporting as possible, with a vegetable garden, orchard, bees, goats, sheep and poultry to supply some of our food needs. We have also tried to use alternative energy sources, where possible. Similarly, we have done most of our own building.

From time to time, we may leave to preach, give a lecture, or do work of some kind, but the desire to return to our place is fundamental to our spirituality. The brothers seek to remember that prayer is the foundation of their every activity. We aim to acquire a constant sense of God's presence, and nurture our relationship with Christ by daily prayer together and in solitude.

There is no leader of the community. Each brother has responsibility for certain areas of the community's life. Decision-making is by consensus.

Brother Wayne	Brother Geoffrey Adam
Brother Howard	*Novices:* 1

Community Publication

Bush Telegraph. Contact the Little Brothers for a subscription which is by donation.

Community Wares

Honey, jam, marmalade, hand-painted cards.

Guest and Retreat Facilities

There is a guest cabin for one - or two 'at a push'.

Associates

These are friends who support the brothers and follow a simple Rule of Life, and for whom the brothers pray.

The Melanesian Brotherhood

MBH

Founded 1925

Solomon Islands Region
The Motherhouse of the Melanesian Brotherhood
Tabalia
PO Box 1479
Honiara
Solomon Islands

Papua New Guinea Region
Good Shepherd Regional Headquarters
Haruro
PO Box 29
Popondetta
Oro Province
Papua New Guinea

Southern Region
Tumsisiro Regional Headquarters
PO Box 05
Lolowai
Ambae
Vanuatu

The Melanesian Brotherhood was founded by Ini Kopuria, a native Solomon Islander from Guadalcanal, in 1925. Its main purpose was evangelistic, to take and live the Gospel in the most remote islands and villages throughout the Solomon Islands, among people who had not heard the message of Christ. The Brotherhood's method is to live as brothers to the people, respecting their traditions and customs: planting, harvesting, fishing, house building, eating and sharing with the people in all these things. Kopuria believed that Solomon Islanders should be converted in a Melanesian way.

Today, the work of the Brotherhood has broadened to include work and mission among both Christians and non-Christians. The Melanesian Brotherhood now has three regions: Solomon Islands, Papua New Guinea, and Vanuatu & Fiji. They have recently opened a house in Palawan, the Philippines.

The Brotherhood aims to live the Gospel in a direct and simple way following Christ's example of prayer, mission and service. The brothers take the vows of poverty, chastity and obedience, but these are not life vows but for a period of five years, which can be renewed. They train for three years as novices and make their vows as brothers at the Feast of St Simon and St Jude.

Brother Caulton Waris MBH
(*Leader of all three regions, assumed office October 1995*)

Professed Brothers: 300
(Solomon Islands: 200; PNG: 90; Southern Region: 20)
Novices: 150
(Solomon Islands: 100; PNG: 30; Southern Region: 20)

Community Publication
Spearhead TokTok, published twice a year, price 25p.

Community History
Brian Macdonald Milne, *Spearhead: the Story of the Melanesian Brotherhood,* is a short history, available from the author, price £2.00, from 39 Way Lane, Waterbeach, Cambridge CB5 9NQ.

Guest and Retreat Facilities
Chester Resthouse, PO Box 1479, Honiara, Solomon Islands, offers a Christian welcome. Eight twin-bedded rooms, self-catering, £10 per room per night.
All the Brotherhood's headquarters and section headquar-

Timetable of the Main House:

First Office and Mattins
5.50 am
(6.20 am Sun & holidays)

Holy Communion
6.15 am
(7.15 am on Sun & holidays)

Morning Office
8.00 am

Midday Office
12 noon
(Angelus on Sun & holidays)

Afternoon Office
1.30 pm
(not Sun & holidays)

Evensong
5.30 pm
(6.00 pm Sun & holidays)

Last Office
9.00 pm

Office Book: Offices and Prayers of the Melanesian Brotherhood 1996

(not for public sale)

ters can provide simple accommodation for visitors. Retreats can be made by prior arrangement with the Chaplain.

Companions

The Melanesian Brotherhood is supported both in prayer, in their work and materially by the Companions of the Melanesian Brotherhood.

For more information about becoming a Companion, please contact:

in the UK
Revd Brian Macdonald Milne
39 Way Lane
Waterbeach
Cambridge CB5 9NQ
UK

in the Solomon Islands
Companions Secretary
PO Box 1479
Honiara
SOLOMON ISLANDS

SOLOMON ISLANDS REGION

BROTHER GEORGE SIOSI MBH
(*Regional Leader, assumed office October 1995*)

Central Section

1. Norman Palmer Household, Honiara
2. St Barnabas Working Household, Honiara
3. Bishopsdale Working Household, Honiara
4. Thomas Peo Working Household, Gela
5. Ini Kopiura Household, Kolina, Guadalcanal
6. Olimauri Working Household, Babanakira, Guadalcanal
7. Calvary Household, Surapau, Guadalcanal
8. Selwyn Rapu Working Household, Talibau, Guadalcanal
9. Derick Vagi Working Household, Bellona
10. David Sale Working Household, Komukama

Malaita Section

11. Airahu Section Headquarters, Malaita
12. Funakawa Household, East Kwaio, Malaita
13. Apalolo Household, Small Malaita
14. John Falea Working Household, Are'Are, Malaita
15. New Dawn Range Working Household, West Kwaio
16. Manao'oba Working Household, North Malaita

Ysabel Section

17. Welchman Section Headquarters, Sosilo, Ysabel
18. Porophetta Household, Kia, Ysabel
19. Lawe Household, Gizo, Western Province

20. Hulon Working Household, Yandina, Russel Islands

Hanuato'o Section
21. Fox Section Headquarters, Makira
22. Ullawa Working Household, Ullawa Island
23. Star Harbour Working Household, Makira
24. Hanunu Working Household, Makira

Temotu Section
25. Makio Section Headquarters, Santa Cruz, Temotu

PAPUA NEW GUINEA REGION

BROTHER ROBIN LINDSAY MBH
(*Regional Leader, assumed office October 1995*)

Popondetta Section
1. Waseta Household
2. Wanigela Household
3. Domara Household
4. Berubona Household
5. Nidewari Working Household

Aiporongo Section
6. Aiome Section Headquarters
7. Kinibong Household
8. Aum Household
9. Kuiama Household

Port Moresby Section
15. Cape Rodney Section Headquarters
16. Pivo Household, Kerema
17. Sogeri Household

SOUTHERN REGION

BROTHER THOMAS MARTOK MBH
(*Regional Leader, assumed office October 1995*)

1. Suriau Household, Santo Bush, VANUATU
2. Port Patteson Household, Vureas Bay, Banks and Torres Section, VANUATU
3. Nabatolu Household, Ba, PO Box 248, FIJI

PHILIPPINES
1. Northern Palawan Christian Institute, Winigit, Paglaum, Taytay, 5312 Palawan
2. IFI Church, Espanola, 5305, Palawan

Oratory of the Good Shepherd

OGS

Founded 1913

The Oratory of the Good Shepherd is a society of priests and laymen founded at Cambridge (UK), which now has provinces in North America, Australia, Southern Africa and Great Britain.

Oratorians are bound together by a common Rule and discipline; members do not generally live together in community. The brethren are grouped in 'colleges' and meet regularly for prayer and support, and each province meets annually for retreat and chapter. Every three years, the General Chapter meets, presided over by the Superior of the whole Oratory, whose responsibility is to maintain the unity of the provinces.

Consecration of life in the Oratory has the twin purpose of fostering the individual brother's personal search for God in union with his brethren, and as a sign of the Kingdom. So through the apostolic work of the brethren, the Oratory seeks to make a contribution to the life and witness of the whole Church.

In common with traditional communities, the Oratory requires celibacy. Brothers are accountable to their brethren for their spending and are expected to live simply and with generosity. The ideal spiritual pattern includes daily Eucharist, Offices, and an hour of prayer. Study is also regarded as important in the life. During this time, the new brother is cared for and nurtured in the Oratory life by another brother of his College. The brother may then, with the consent of the province, make his first profession, which is renewed annually for at least five years, though with the hope of intention and perseverance for life. After five years, profession can be made for a longer period, and after ten years a brother may, with the consent of the whole Oratory, make his profession for life.

THE RIGHT REVEREND JOHN SALT OGS
Bishop of St Helena
(Superior)

The Community in Australia

KEITH DEAN-JONES OGS (*Provincial*)
The Rectory, 7 Thomas Street, Cardiff, NSW 2285
AUSTRALIA
Tel: 2 4954 8550

Ronald Henderson	Kenneth Mason
Michael Chiplin	Barry Greaves
Charles Helms	Robert Braun
Geoffrey Tisdall	Trevor Bulled
Michael Boyle	Bruce Falconer

The Community in North America

CARLSON GERDAU OGS (*Provincial*)
Apt 19 A/N, 60 Sutton Place South, New York, NY 10022, USA
Tel: 212 421 6942 *E-Mail: cgerdau@ogs.net*

Martin Davidson
Victor Preller
Henry Hill
Philip Hobson
Wally Raymond
William Derby

Probationers: 1

The Community in Southern Africa

JOHN SALT OGS (*Superior & Provincial*)
PO Box 62, St Helena, South Atlantic Ocean
Fax: 290 4330

John Ruston
David Bailey
Mark Vandeyar
David Johnson
Thami Shangi
Probationers: 1

The Community in the UK

LINDSAY URWIN OGS
(Provincial, assumed office 1996)
Bishop's House, 21 Guildford Road, Horsham, RH12 1LU, UK
Tel: 01403 211139 *Fax: 01403 217349* *E-Mail: bishhorsham@clara.net*

George Briggs
Brian Oman
Robert Symonds
John Thorold
David Jowitt
Michael Bootes
Peter Ford
Michael Bartlett
David Johnson
Dominic Walker
Clive McCleester
Malcolm King
James Finnemore
Brian Lee
Michael Bullock
Christopher Powell
Michael Longstaffe
Nicholas Gandy

Probationers: 1

Obituaries

2 Apr 1998	Thomas Gresley Summers, aged 73, professed 36 years
2 Jun 1998	Geoffrey Kentigern Bostock, aged 67, professed 7 years
24 May 1999	George Basil Braund, aged 72, professed 47 years

Companions and Associates

The Oratory has an extended family of Companions, with their own rule of life, and Associates. Companionship is open to men and women, lay or ordained, married or single.

Community History

George Tibbatts, *The Oratory of the Good Shepherd: The First Seventy-five Years*, The Almoner OGS, Windsor, 1988.

Order of the Holy Cross

OHC

Founded 1884

Mount Calvary
PO Box 1296
Santa Barbara
CA 93102
USA
Tel: 805 963 8175

Mount Calvary Retreat House
Tel: 805 962 9855

Holy Cross Monastery & Novitiate
PO Box 99
West Park
NY 12493
USA
Tel: 914 384 6660

Holy Cross Priory
204 High Park Avenue
Toronto
Ontario M6P 2S6
CANADA
Tel: 416 767 9081

Incarnation Priory
1601 Oxford Street
Berkeley
CA 94709
USA
Tel: 510 548 3406

The Order of the Holy Cross is a contemporary Benedictine monastic community open to both clergymen and laymen. The principles which govern the Order's life are in two documents: The Rule, written by James Otis Sargent Huntington, the founder of the Order, and the Rule of St Benedict.

The liturgical life of each house centers around the corporate praying of the Daily Office and the celebration of the Holy Eucharist. Members also spend time in private prayer and meditation.

The work of the Order is varied, as members are encouraged to find ways to use their own unique talents in ministry. Houses of the Order vary from traditional monastic retreat/conference centers of hospitality to active inner-city urban houses. Members of the Order are engaged in preaching, counseling and spiritual direction, in teaching, in parish work, in evangelism, in retreat work, and in ministry to alcoholics, addicts and those with AIDS. The Order has a special ministry of building the monastic life in the Anglican Church in Africa.

For further information on vocation or any other matter write:

WILLIAM SIBLEY OHC
(*Superior*)

at the Mount Calvary address.

Community Publication
Holy Cross, published three times a year.

Community History
Adam Dunbar McCoy OHC, *Holy Cross: A Century of Anglican Monasticism*, Morehouse-Barlow, Wilton, CT, 1987.

Associates
Associated with the Order are groups of clergy and lay people who participate in varying degrees in the prayer and work of Holy Cross. Information about these groups can be had by writing any of the houses.

***

uMariya uMama weThemba Monastery and Novitiate,
PO Box 6013, Grahamstown 6141,
SOUTH AFRICA
Tel: 46 633 8111

Order of the Holy Paraclete

OHP

Founded 1915

St Hilda's Priory
Sneaton Castle
Whitby
North Yorkshire
YO21 3QN
UNITED KINGDOM

Tel: 01947 602079
Fax: 01947 820854
E-Mail: ohpprioryWhitby@btinternet.com

Morning Prayer
7.15 am
(7.25 am Sat,
7.30 am Sun)

Midday Office
12.15 pm
(12 noon Sat)

Mass
12.30 pm
(8.00 am Sat,
9.30 am Sun)

Vespers
5.30 pm
(4.30 pm Fri)

Compline
9.00 pm
(informal on Fri)

Office Book:
OHP Office

Registered Charity:
No. 271117

Although founded as an educational Order, the Sisters have now diversified their work to include hospitality, development work overseas, inner city involvement, retreats and spiritual direction. The mother house of the Order is at St Hilda's Priory, Sneaton Castle, Whitby. Some Sisters work in Sneaton Castle Centre, adjacent to the Priory, which caters for day and residential groups - pilgrimages, parish holidays, school visits, field courses, music workshop etc. There are houses in Ghana, South Africa and Swaziland as well as in Leicester, York, Rievaulx, Dundee and Boston Spa (Martin House Children's Hospice). Central to the Order's life are the Divine Office and Eucharist, a strong emphasis on corporate activity, and a lively interest in the Celtic Church and the early saints of Northern Britain.

SISTER JUDITH OHP
(Prioress, assumed office 8 May 1998)
SISTER BARBARA ANN OHP (*Sub-Prioress*)

Sister Bridget Mary
Sister Kathleen
Sister Mary Dorothea
Sister Barbara
Sister Eileen
Sister Mary
Sister Rachel
Sister Ursula
Sister Barbara Maude
Sister Sophia
Sister Margaret Irene
Sister Bertha
Sister Olive
Sister Francis Clare
Sister Marjorie
Sister Rosa
Sister Rosalind
Sister Constance
Sister Catherine
Sister Sheila
Sister Janet
Sister Philippa
Sister Alison
Sister Alicia
Sister Michelle
Sister Truda
Sister Mary Nina
Sister Stella Mary
Sister Lucy
Sister Naomi
Sister Heather
Sister Muriel
Sister Mary Margaret
Sister Anita
Sister Margaret Shirley
Sister Hilary
Sister Nancye
Sister Patricia
Sister Gillian
Sister Hilary Joy
Sister Maureen
Sister Grace
Sister Janette
Sister Janet Elizabeth
Sister Betty
Sister Marion
Sister Dorothy Stella
Sister Benedicta
Sister Caroline
Sister Margaret Elizabeth
Sister Marion Eva
Sister Heather Francis
Sister Erika
Sister Maureen Ruth
Sister Margaret Anne
Sister Jocelyn

Sister Carole
Sister Mavis
Sister Kate
Sister Rachel Clare
Sister Linda
Sister Aba
Sister Pam
Sister Helen
Novices: 3

Obituaries

5 Mar 1998	Sister Mary Francis, aged 89, professed 62 years
8 Apr 1998	Sister Birgit, aged 77, professed 34 years
20 May 1998	Sister Beatrice, aged 81, professed 52 years
21 Aug 1998	Sister Susan, aged 54, professed 18 years
28 Sep 1998	Sister Jean, aged 80, professed 51 years

Houses in the UK

Martin House
Grove Road
Clifford
Wetherby LS23 6TX
Tel: 01937 843449
E-Mail: sisters.martinhs@onet.co.uk

Beach Cliff
14 North Promenade
Whitby
N Yorks YO21 3JX
Tel: 01947 601968

St Oswald's Pastoral Centre
Woodlands Drive
Sleights, Whitby
N Yorks YO21 1RY
Tel: 01947 810496
Fax: 01947 810750
E-Mail: ohpstos@globalnet.co.uk

St Michael's House
15 Portman Street
Belgrave
Leicester LE14 6NZ
Tel: 0116 266 7805 *Fax: 0116 268 0374*
E-Mail: sistersohp@Leicester.anglican.org

The Abbey Cottage
Rievaulx
York YO62 5LB
Tel: 01439 798209

7 Minster Yard
York YO1 7JD
Tel: 01904 620601

St Hilda's House
20 Craigielea Place
Dundee DD4 8HL
Tel: 01328 509206

Houses in Africa

PO Box 594
Accra
GHANA
Tel: 21 556675

PO Box 3811
Manzini
SWAZILAND
Tel & Fax: 50 57222
E-Mail: jdean@lafrica.sz

St Hilda's House,
PO Box 1272
Manzini
SWAZILAND
Tel: 50 53323
Fax: 50 54083

St Benedict's Retreat House
PO Box 27
Rosettenville 2130
SOUTH AFRICA
Tel: 011 435 3662
Fax: 011 435 2970
E-Mail: stben@cpsa.or.za

Community Publication
OHP Newsletter, twice a year. Write to The Publications Secretary at St Hilda's Priory. The cost is under review.

Community History
A Foundation Member, *Fulfilled in Joy*, Hodder & Stoughton, 1964.
Brief History of the Order of the Holy Paraclete, published by OHP.

Community Wares
Cards and crafts.

Guest and Retreat Facilities
St Hilda's Priory: nine rooms (six single; two double; one twin) in the Priory or nearby houses. Individuals or small groups are welcome for personal quiet or retreat, day or residential. If asked for in advance, some guidance can be provided. There is no programme of retreats at the Priory. Write to the Guest Sister with enquiries and bookings.

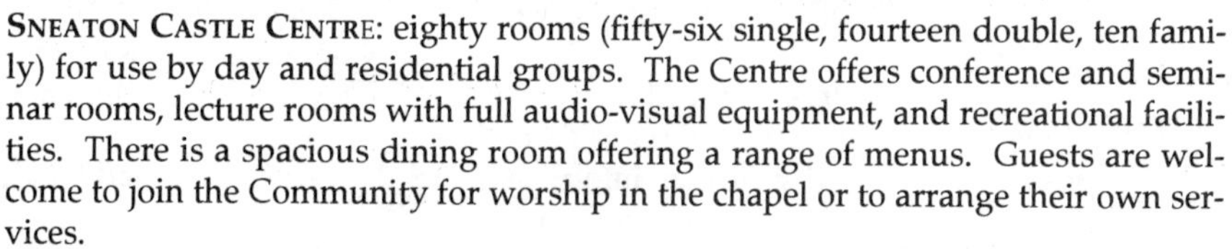

Sneaton Castle Centre: eighty rooms (fifty-six single, fourteen double, ten family) for use by day and residential groups. The Centre offers conference and seminar rooms, lecture rooms with full audio-visual equipment, and recreational facilities. There is a spacious dining room offering a range of menus. Guests are welcome to join the Community for worship in the chapel or to arrange their own services.
Contact the Bookings Secretary, Sneaton Castle Centre, Whitby YO21 3QN.

St Oswald's Pastoral Centre: twelve rooms (eight single, four twin). Amenities include a chapel, two lounges, a small library and a kitchen where guests can make hot drinks. Full catering is provided. A separate facility, the Grimston Room, can hold about thirty people for quiet days or conferences. An annual programme of Open Events is published in *Retreats* and is available on request: groups and individuals are welcome at times. Enquiries and bookings to the Sister-in-charge.

Tertiaries and Associates
The OHP Tertiary Order is a fellowship of women and men, united under a common discipline, based on the OHP Rule, and supporting one another in their discipleship. Tertiaries are ordinary Christians seeking to offer their lives in the service of Christ, helping the Church and showing love in action. They value their links with each other and with the Sisters of the Order, at Whitby and elsewhere, and when possible they meet together for mutual support in prayer, discussion and ministry. The Tertiary Order is open to communicant members of any Trinitarian Church.

The OHP Associates are friends of the Order who desire to keep in touch with its life and work while serving God in their various spheres. Many have made initial contact with the Sisters through a visit or parish mission, or via another Associate. All are welcome, married or single, clergy or lay, regardless of religious affiliation.

Order of Julian of Norwich

OJN

Founded 1985

S10 W26392 Summit Avenue, Waukesha WI 53188-2636 USA

Tel: 414 549 0452
Fax: 414 549 0670
E-Mail: Ordjulian@aol.com

Morning Prayer
6.00 am

Mass
7.00 am

Noonday Office
12 noon

Evensong
5.00 pm

Compline
8.30 pm

Office Book: The Book of Common Prayer of the Episcopal Church of the USA for Morning Prayer; OJN Chantbook for other Offices

Wisconsin Tax Exempt No. : ES-31183

The Order of Julian of Norwich is a semi-enclosed contemplative monastic community of Episcopalians, living under the traditional vows, in the spirit of Dame Julian of Norwich, the fourteenth-century English anchoress and mystic. The Order revives the medieval practice of including *both* monks and nuns under the same vows, with equal status in the same order. Founded in 1985, its apostolate is the practice, teaching, and promulgation of classical Christian contemplative prayer, retreats, spiritual direction, study, and writing.

The life of prayer is lived on an axis between the oratory and the personal cell, and includes the four-fold Divine Office of the Book of Common Prayer, daily Eucharist, and the daily practice of personal contemplative prayer. Gregorian chant is normally used for Noonday Office, Evensong and Compline. The formation process takes approximately four years before Solemn Life Vows.

The Order is affiliated with the Conference on Religious Life in the Anglican Communion in the Americas, and is canonically recognized by the Committee on Religious Orders of the House of Bishops of the Episcopal Church in the United States of America.

For further information on the Order or its affiliates, address the Guardian.

THE REVD SISTER SCHOLASTICA MARIE BURTON OJN
(*Sister Guardian, assumed office September 1995*)
THE REVD FATHER GREGORY FRUEHWIRTH OJN (*Warden*)
Father John-Julian Swanson
Sister Cornelia Barry
Sister Monica Clark
Sister Clare Carbone
Sister Hilary Crupi
Novices: 2

Community Publication

JuliaNews (newsletter) & *Julian Jottings (essays)* both bi-monthly. Subscription free. Contact Sister Monica OJN.

Community History

Teunisje Velthuizen, *One-ed into God: The first decade of the Order of St Julian of Norwich,* The Julian Press, 1996.

Community Wares

The Julian Shop has books, religious articles, many pamphlets written by members.

Guest and Retreat Facilities

Two guest rooms. There is no charge.

Associates and Oblates
ASSOCIATES Friends of the Order who keep a simple Rule (one daily Office, Sunday Mass, annual reports to the Warden of Associates) and pledge financial support for the Order.
OBLATES They have a demanding Rule of: two BCP Offices daily; three per cent of their income to the Order, seven per cent of their income to their parish or to charity; three hours contemplative prayer a week; four-day silent retreat annually; Sunday Mass; seven Holy days of Obligation, etc. They make a semi-annual report to the Warden of Oblates.

Order of St Anne at Bethany

OSA

Founded 1910

25 Hillside Avenue
Arlington
MA 02476
USA

Tel: 781 643 0921

We are a small multi-cultural community of women committed to witnessing to the truth that, as Christians, we belong to this age, this society; and that it is here and now that we demonstrate to the Church and the world that Religious Life lived in community is relevant, interesting, fulfilling and needed in our world and our times.

We are four Filipinas, one American and one Bahamian, and we strive to recognize and value such a diversity of persons and gifts.

We believe that God has a vision for each one of us and that opportunities to serve the Church and the world are abundant. For this to become real, we know that our spirits and hearts must be enlarged to fit the dimensions of our Church in today's world.

If our dedication and witness as Religious are to mean anything at all then we will always be seeking and exploring new ways of service to the wider community, both as individual disciples and as women living together in community.

The Rule of the Order of St Anne says *our houses may be small, but our hearts are larger than houses.* Our community has from its founding been 'people-oriented' - although this expression was unknown at the time. We derive a sense of joy and satisfaction in offering hospitality both at the Convent, at St John's House, and in our beautiful chapel.

Always constant in our lives are our personal prayer and corporate worship: our vows of Poverty, Celibacy and Obedience, our commitment to spiritual growth and development of mind and talents, and our fellowship with one another as friends and sisters.

Order of St Benedict

Alton Abbey

OSB

Founded 1884

Alton Abbey
Abbey Road
Beech, Alton
Hampshire
GU34 4AP
UK
Tel: 01420 562145
& 563575
Fax: 01420 561691

The Vigil
5.30 am

Morning Prayer
7.15 am

Mass
9.00 am
(10 am Sun & Solemnities)

Midday Prayer
12.00 noon

Evening Prayer
5.00 pm

Night Prayer
8.30 pm (7.30 pm Sun)

Office Book:
Alton Abbey Office book

Registered Charity:
No. 229216

The Community, now dedicated to Our Lady and Saint John, was founded on the work undertaken among sailors in Burma and India from 1884 by the Revd Charles Plomer Hopkins. From 1896, the Community concentrated its activities at the mother house at Alton (1895 to the present), with priories also at Barry (1894-1912) and Greenwich (1899-1951). The active work among seamen was discontinued in 1989; the Community continues to administer the Seamen's Friendly Society as a charitable trust. Having observed the Rule of St Benedict from 1893, the Community formally adopted the Rule on 28 January 1981, when new constitutions received ratification from the Visitor.

RT REVD DOM GILES HILL OSB
(Abbot, elected 12 September 1990)
VERY REVD DOM WILLIAM HUGHES OSB *(Prior)*

Revd Dom Peter Roundhill
Dom Andrew Johnson
Revd Dom Nicholas Seymour *(Novice Master)*
Dom Stephen Hoare
Dom Anselm Shobrook
Rt Revd Timothy Bavin
Brother Phillip Hickman

Community Publication
The Messenger, occasional, write to the Abbey.

Guest and Retreat Facilities
Guest house facilities for up to eighteen persons, for both group and individual retreats. There is a programme of retreats each year, which is available from the Guestmaster.

Most convenient time to telephone: 4.00 pm - 4.30 pm.

Community Wares
Altar bread department: contact Dom Stephen Hoare.

Oblates
For details of the Oblates of St Benedict, please contact the Oblate Master.

Website:
http://www.btinternet.com/~nbch/Abbey.html

Order of St Benedict

Bartonville

OSB

Founded 1985

Abbey of Saint Benedict, 7561 West Lancaster Road
Bartonville
Illinois 61607
USA
Tel: 309 633 0057
Fax: 309 633 0058
E-Mail: sbabbey@ocslink.com

The Office of Readings and Morning Prayer, followed by Mass
6.30 am

Sext
12 noon

Noon Office
3.00 pm

Evening Prayer followed by Meditation
5.00 pm

Compline
8.30 pm

Sunday Mass
10.00 am (English)
3.00 pm (Spanish)

The Community was founded on 15 August 1985 at San Juan in Puerto Rico, as a Spanish-speaking Ecumenical Benedictine House. They concentrate upon the Divine Office, daily Mass and praying for unity and reconciliation of the Church of Christ. What work they do for the Church is mainly done within the monastery, such as retreats and spiritual direction. However, they have also led retreats throughout the United States in parishes and convents and other retreat houses. In May 1996, the community moved from Puerto Rico to Bartonville, Illinois. In September 1998, they purchased an additional fifteen-acre property to supply the needs for additional retreatants. They have been affiliated to Alton Abbey in the UK since 1995.

RT REVD DOM J ALBERTO MORALES OSB
(Abbot, elected 1991)
Revd Dom Trevor Rhodes
Revd Dom Luis Gonzalez (*Administrator*)
Revd Dom Harold Camacho (*Oblate Director*)
Dom Pedro Escabi Agostini
Revd James Marshall (*Oblate-in-residence and Guestmaster*)

Novices: 1 *Postulants:* 2

Community Publication
Abbey News, published quarterly.

Guest and Retreat Facilities
There are guest facilities for up to twenty persons.

Community Wares
Church goods and religious articles: Abbey incense, Abbey coffee (imported from Puerto Rico) and Abbey fruit cake.

Oblates
For details of the Oblates of St Benedict, please contact the Oblate Master.

Website: http://www.ocslink.com/~sbabbey

Office Book
The community uses its own Benedictine Office book.

Order of St Benedict

Burford Priory

OSB

Founded 1941

Priory of Our Lady
Priory Lane, Burford
Oxfordshire
OX18 4SQ
UK
Tel: 01993 823605

Lauds
6.45 am
(7.00 am Sun & Solemnities)

Terce
9.00 am

Eucharist
12.00 noon (10.30 am Sun)

None
2.00 pm

Vespers
5.30 pm

Compline
9.00 pm
(8.30 pm, Sat & Sun & Eve of Solemnities Vigil)

Office Book:
Burford Office

Registered Charity:
No. 221617

The Priory is home to a mixed Community of nuns and monks who live a shared life under the Rule of St Benedict, observing a balance between prayer, study and manual work. Members of the Community do not normally undertake outside engagements, but help to support themselves by their ministry of hospitality at the Community's small retreat and guest house and by various works undertaken within the enclosure. They are largely responsible themselves for the upkeep of the Priory, its extensive garden, grounds and woodland.

VERY REVD BROTHER STUART BURNS OSB
(Prior, elected 14 October 1996)

Sister Scholastica Newman
Sister Mary Bernard Taylor
Brother Thomas Quin *(Novice Guardian)*
Brother Anthony Hare
Brother Philip Dulson

Novices: 1
Postulants: 1

Guest and Retreat Facilities
Eight-bedroomed retreat house, with four single rooms and four twin-bedded rooms.

Community Wares
Block mounted icon prints.
Mounted photograph cards.
Printing (hand press) cards and letter heads.

Oblates and Friends
There is a small group of Oblates and a Friends' Association.

Order of St Benedict

OSB

Camperdown

Founded 1975

Benedictine Monastery
PO Box 111
Camperdown
Victoria 3260
AUSTRALIA

Tel & Fax:
3 559 323448

Vigils 4.30 am

Lauds 6.30 am

Terce & Conventual Mass 8.15 am

Sext 11.45 am

None 2.10 pm

Vespers 5.00 pm

Compline 7.30 pm

Office Book: Camperdown breviary with a two-week cycle of the Psalter & seasonal variations.

The Community was founded in the parish of St Mark the Evangelist in Melbourne on 8 November 1975, when the first two monks were clothed. In 1980, after working in this inner city parish for five years, and after adopting the Rule of Saint Benedict, they moved to the country town of Camperdown. Here the Community lives a contemplative monastic life with the emphasis on the balanced life of prayer and work that forms the Benedictine ethos. In 1993, the Chapter decided to admit women and to endeavour to establish a mixed community of monks and nuns. To this end, two nuns came from Malling Abbey (UK) and one has transferred her stability to Camperdown. The Community supports itself through the operation of a printery, icon reproduction, crafts and a small guest house. A permanent monstery has now been built and the monastery church was consecrated by the diocesan bishop in February 1995.

THE VERY REVD DOM MICHAEL KING OSB
(*Prior, installed 21 March 1980*)
SISTER MARY PHILIP BLOORE OSB (*Sub-Prior*)
Dom Placid Lawson
Oblate Sister Mary John Winterbotham
Postulants: 2

Community publication
The Community produces a newsletter at Christmas and in July.

Community Wares
Icons; printing.

Guest and Retreat Facilities
There is a small guest house, open to men and women, for private retreats and spiritual direction.

Oblates
There is a small group of clerics and lay people who form the Oblates of the community following the Benedictine life according to their particular status.

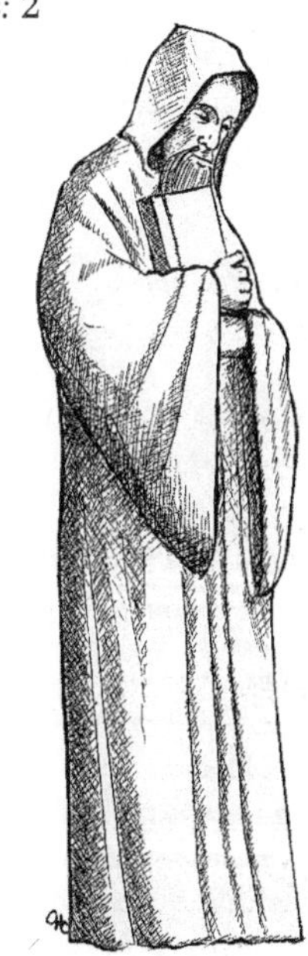

St Benedict,
drawn by a sister CHC

Order of St Benedict

Community of St Mary at the Cross, Edgware

OSB

Founded 1866

St Mary at the Cross
Priory Field Drive
Hale Lane
Edgware
Middlesex HA8 9PZ
UK

Tel: 0208 958 7868
Fax: 0208 958 1920

Readings and Lauds
7.00 am (7.30 am Sun)

Midday Office
11.55 am (except Sun)

Vespers 5.30 pm
(4.40 pm Fri)

Compline 7.30 pm

Mass
7.45 am weekdays
11.00 am once a week
11.00 am Sun & feast days

The Anglo-Catholic movement was at its height and the revival of Religious Life in the Church of England was in full swing, when the Community began its life in Shoreditch. "Let the end of your being be God ... ", wrote Revd Henry Nihill, co-founder of the Community with Mother Monnica Skinner. Prayer and worship through the offering of the Divine Office and the Eucharist were to be the heart of its life.

Worship found expression in loving care, as the sisters responded to the desperate needs of the sick, poor and disabled around them. This work grew and continued, developing to meet the needs and demands of its time, changing from the simplicity and poverty of a shared community life to the provision today of a high-quality modern Nursing Home, Henry Nihill House, in Edgware.

The abbey at Edgware is seen as a haven of peace which enfolds its many visitors. Guests are offered Benedictine hospitality with space for rest and renewal, and the opportunity to share in the Community's offering of the Divine Office and Eucharist, which remains central to its life.

RT REVD DAME MARY THÉRÈSE ZELENT OSB
(Abbess, elected 30 March 1993)
VERY REVD DAME MARY EANFLEDA BARBARA JOHNSON OSB
(Prioress)
Dame Rosemary Francis Breeze
Dame Raphael Mary Pay
(Former Superior, Servants of Christ)
Dame Dorothea Mary Haviland
Dame Teresa Mary Hastie
Dame Jane Frances Franklin

Intern Oblate: Raili Lappalainen

Novices: 1

Ethiopian Orthodox:
Sister Atsede Bekele Sister Tirsit Eguale

Community Publication
Abbey Newsletter, published yearly. There is no charge but donations are welcome. Obtainable from the Convent.

Community Wares
CLOISTER CRAFTS
A good selection of books, icons, attractive hand-crafted goods of all kinds are available, plus a varied range of cards for most occasions.

Holy Hour:
4.40 pm on Fri
(Vespers and Benediction)

First Fri of month:
11.55 am
Exposition and prayer, ending in Holy Hour.

Office Book:
The Divine Office.
The Community has its own form of Compline.

Registered Charity:
No. 209261

Guest and Retreat Facilities

Only minutes from the M1, the Convent offers an excellent:

Day Conference Centre

Open 9 am - 6 pm, the Centre has space for about fifty people: ideal for church groups, training days, family parties etc. It is fully wheel-chair accessible. Closed Holy Week and the Christmas holiday.

Guest accommodation

Loreto - a small comfortable guest house with seven bedrooms. Hospitality for up to seven days for rest and retreat.

Hermitage - a one-bedroom flatlet, self-contained but not self-catering, which is ideal for a time of real quiet.

Quiet Days - a welcome is given to anyone needing space in their lives for prayer, study or reflection.

Please note that there is a recommended tariff which covers basic costs for guest facilities etc. but special arrangements can be made with Mother Abbess for anyone who cannot afford these costs.

Requests for booking forms may be made by telephone, Monday-Friday, 9.00 am - 4.30 pm, or by post to the Guest Mistress.

Oblates

Our Oblates are part of our extended Community family: living outside the cloister; following the spirit of the Holy Rule of St Benedict; bonded with the Community in prayer and commitment to service.

Prayer Link

Many people, often whole parishes, are linked with the Community in a simple commitment to prayer and intercession.

Monastic experience

Applications are considered from women who wish to spend up to three months living alongside the Community and sharing in its life and worship. (There is no long-term accommodation for men.)

Order of St Benedict

Elmore Abbey

OSB

Founded 1914

Elmore Abbey
Church Lane
Speen, Newbury
Berkshire RG14 1SA
UK

Tel: 01635 33080

Vigils	*5.30 am*
Lauds	*8.00 am*
Terce	*10.00 am*
Sext	*12.00 noon*
None	*4.00 pm*
Vespers	*6.00 pm*
Compline	*8.30 pm*

Mass:
8.00 am Mon - Sat (with Lauds)
10.30 am Sun (Parish Church)

Registered Charity : Pershore Nashdom & Elmore Trust - No. 220012

The monastery aims to provide an environment within which the traditional monastic balance between worship, study and work may be maintained with a characteristic Benedictine stress upon corporate worship and community life. To this end, outside commitments are kept to a minimum.

RT REVD DOM BASIL MATTHEWS OSB
(Abbot, elected 3 July 1988)
VERY REVD DOM FRANCIS HUTCHISON OSB *(Prior)*

Revd Dom Boniface Nielsen
Dom Mark Alberic Brierly
Rt Revd Dom Kenneth Newing (*Novice Master*)
Dom Simon Jarrett (*Sub Prior*)
Dom Bruce De Walt
Brother Hugh Kelly
Brother Paul Fenton
Father Patrick Phelan

Community Publication
Elmore Abbey Record, yearly, write to the Cellarer.
Books:
Augustine Morris, *Oblates: Life with Saint Benedict* £4.25.
Simon Bailey, *A Tactful God: Gregory Dix,* £12.99.

Community Wares
Incense: 500g packets made at the Abbey.
Brands: Glastonbury £8; Rievaulx £7.25; Evesham £7.50; Sherborne £7;
Charcoal: Swift light, 80 small rings £5.25.

Prayer stools, fixed and folding: £25.00
Pricket stand (as in the Elmore Oratory): price on request.
Contact: The Cellarer, Elmore Abbey.

Guest and Retreat Facilities
There is a small guest house with accommodation for up to four wishing to stay for a personal retreat or period of quiet. Guests are admitted to the Oratory, the Guests' Common Room, the Refectory and the front garden.

Oblates
An extended confraternity of oblates, numbering 330 men and women, married and single, seek to live according to a rule of life inspired by Benedictine principles. From the start, the community has believed in the importance of prayer for Christian unity and the fostering of ecumenism. Details can be obtained from the Oblate Master.

Order of St Benedict

Malling Abbey OSB

Founded 1891

St Mary's Abbey
52 Swan Street
West Malling
Kent
ME19 6JX
UK

Tel: 01732 843309

Vigils
4.30 am (5.00 am Sun)

Lauds
6.50 am (8.10 am Sun)

Eucharist
7.30 am (9.00 am Sun)

Terce 8.35 am

Sext 12.00 noon

None 3.00 pm

Vespers 4.45 pm

Compline 7.25 pm

Office Book:
Malling Abbey Office

Saint Benedict sees the monastery as a school of the Lord's service where a united community endeavours to grow in stability, conversion of life and obedience within the enclosure. The call of God is the essential requirement for admission to the novitiate to share in the life of prayer, study and manual work in the house and grounds. The period of training before final profession is normally five and a half years.

MOTHER ABBESS MARY JOHN MARSHALL OSB
(elected 27 September 1990)
SISTER MARY PAUL COLLINS OSB *(Prioress)*

M Perpetua Towell
Sr Mary Augustine Dalgarno
Sr Macrina Banner
Sr Martina Michael
Sr Anastasia Feast
Sr Mary Gregory Barrett
Sr Mary Mark Brooksbank
Sr Mary Ignatius Conklin
Sr Mary Simon Corbett
Sr Ruth Blackmore
Sr Mary Cuthbert Archer
Sr Mary Francis Tillard
Sr Mary Anselm Topley
Sr Mary Gundulf Wood
Sr Mary David Best
Sr Anna Bowes
Sr Mary Stephen Packwood
Sr Felicity Spencer
Sr Gabriel Allatt
Sr Bartimaeus Ives
Sr Raphael Stone
Sr Seonaid Crabtree
Sr Alison Buttolph
Sr Mary Magdalen Long
Sr Mary Michael Wilson
Sr Miriam Noke
Junior professed: 2
Novices: 1

Community Wares
There are cards and booklets printed and painted at the abbey on sale at the Guest House.

Guest and Retreat Facilities
We offer no organised retreats apart from those for our oblates. Those wishing to make a private retreat are welcome to do so at the Guest House.

Most convenient time to telephone: 7.00 pm - 7.15 pm.

Oblates
Oblates are men and women who feel called by God to follow the Benedictine way, but outside the cloister. They affirm their baptismal commitment by a promise of conversion of life worked out in a personal rule based on Saint Benedict's Rule. They are united to the community and to their fellow oblates in mutual love and fellowship. Oblates share in the community's worship by praying the Office. The minimum is two Offices daily and if possible these are Lauds and Vespers. Eucharist: attendance at least once a week. Retreat: at least two days annually, at the abbey or elsewhere. Regular Prayer and *lectio*. Rule: to be read through at least annually.

Order of St Benedict

Servants of Christ Priory

OSB

Founded 1968

*28 West Pasadena Avenue
Phoenix
AZ 85013 2002
USA*

*Tel & Fax:
602 248 9321*

*Morning Prayer
6.30 am*

*Mass
7.00 am*

*Midday Prayer
Noon*

*Evening Prayer
4.30 pm*

*Compline
8.00 pm*

*Office Book:
The Book of Common Prayer of the Episcopal Church of the USA*

A community united in love for God and one another following the Benedictine balance of prayer, study and work reflects the life of the monks. Outside engagements are accepted as long as they do not interfere with the monastic routine.

THE VERY REVD CORNELIS J. DE RIJK OSB
(*Prior*)
The Revd Lewis H. Long

Novices: 1

Community Wares
We have a gift shop which stocks Prayer Books, hymnals, religious books and jewelry. We also supply altar bread and candles to numerous parishes.

Guest and Retreat Facilities
We have two single rooms and two double rooms for individuals who wish to come and participate in our life. Day guests are also welcome. Guests have use of the grounds, the library, and share meals with the community. We are closed in August.

Oblates
Oblates follow a rule of life consistent with the Rule of St Benedict adapted to their lifestyle. Those in the metropolitan Phoenix area meet once a month at the monastery.

Order of St Benedict Three Rivers OSB

Founded 1939

St Gregory's Abbey
56500 Abbey Road
Three Rivers
Michigan 49093-9595
USA
Tel: 616 244 5893
Fax: 616 244 8712
Website:
http//www2.inetdirect.net/~dburton/osb/

Matins
4.00 am (5.30 am Sun & solemnities, with Lauds)

Lauds
6.00 am

Terce & Mass
8.15 am (8.30 am Sun & solemnities)

Sext
11.30 am (12 noon Sun & solemnities, with None)

None
2.00 pm

Vespers
5.00 pm

Compline
7.45 pm

St Gregory's Abbey is the home of a community of men living under the Rule of St Benedict within the Episcopal Church. The center of the monastery's life is the Abbey Church, where God is worshipped in the daily round of Eucharist, Divine Office, and private prayer. Also offered to God are the monks' daily manual work, study and correspondence, ministry to guests, and occasional outside engagements.

RIGHT REVD ANDREW MARR OSB
(*Abbot, elected 2 March 1989*)
VERY REVD AELRED GLIDDEN OSB (*Prior*)

Father Jude Bell	Brother Abraham Newsom
Father William Forest	
Brother Martin Dalley	*Novices:* 1

Obituaries

9 Oct 1997 Brother Wilfrid Braidi, aged 86, professed 39 years

Community Publications and History

Abbey Newsletter, published four times a year. A subscription is free. To be added to the mailing list, write to the Abbey Business office.

The book *Singing God's Praises* was published in the Fall of 1998. It includes articles from community newsletters over the past sixty years and also includes a history of St Gregory's. Copies can be bought from the Abbey, price $20 a copy, postpaid.

Community Wares

The Abbey sells a calendar each year featuring photographs taken by one of the monks.

Guest and Retreat Facilities

Both men and women are welcome as guests. There is no charge, but $20 per day is 'fair value for services rendered' that is not tax-deductible. For further information and arrangements, contact the guest master by mail, telephone or e-mail at guestga@net-link.net.

Associates

We have a Confraternity which offers an official connection to the Abbey and is open to anyone who wishes to join for the purpose of incorporating Benedictine principles into their lives. For further information and an application form, please write the Father Abbot.

Office Book: The community uses home-made books based on the Roman Thesaurus for the Benedictine Office.

On-Profit Institution Number: 38-1627960

Order of St Helena

OSH

Founded 1945

Convent of St Helena
PO Box 426
Vails Gate
New York 12584
USA

Tel: 914 562 0592
Fax: 914 569 7051
E-Mail:
cintra@ix.netcom.com

Matins
7.00 am
(7.30 am Sat & Sun)

Eucharist
7.30 am
(8.00 am Sat & Sun)

Diurnum
and intercessions
noon

Vespers
5.00 pm

Compline
7.30 pm

Office Book:
OSH Office Book, produced by the sisters in 1990.
It follows closely the Book of Common Prayer of the Episcopal Church of the USA.

The Order of St Helena witnesses to a contemporary version of traditional monasticism, taking a threefold vow of Poverty, Chastity and Obedience. Our life in community is shaped by the daily Eucharist and fourfold Office, plus hours of personal prayer and study, and from this radiates a wide range of ministries.

As an Order, we are not restricted to any single area of work but witness and respond to the Gospel, with individual sisters engaging in different ministries as they feel called by God and affirmed by the community. Our work is thus wonderfully varied: sisters work in parishes as priests or as pastoral assistants; they lead retreats, quiet days and conferences;work with the national Church and various organizations; offer spiritual direction; are psychotherapists; teach; serve in hospital chaplaincies and community service programs. Four sisters are ordained priests.

The convents in Vails Gate, NY, and Augusta, Georgia, have guest houses and offer retreats and conferences.

In 1997, the Order adopted a new style of governance and no longer has a superior or single sister as head. Instead, the Order is led by a four-member Leadership Council, with responsibility and ultimate authority vested equally in all four members.

LEADERSHIP COUNCIL(*assumed office 1997*)

Sister Cintra Pemberton OSH
(*Administrative Officer*)
Sister Ellen Stephen OSH
(*President of Corporation*)
Revd Sister Rosina Ampah OSH
(*Minister of Pastoral Care*)
Sister Linda Julian OSH
(*Minister of Vocations*)

Revd Sister Mary Michael
Sister Clare
Sister Ruth Juchter
Sister Andrea
Sister Cornelia
Revd Sister Jean Campbell
Revd Sister Carol Andrew
Sister Barbara Lee
Sister Benedicta
Sister Elsie
Sister June Thomas
Sister Ann Prentice
Sister Mary Lois
Sister Elena

Addresses of other Houses

Convent of St Helena
PO Box 5645
Augusta
Georgia 30916
USA

Convent of St Helena
134 East 28th Street
New York
New York 10016
USA

Community Publication
saint helena, published quarterly, free of charge. Write to the Convent of St Helena at Vails Gate for a subscription.

Community Wares
Hand-made rosaries - *write to* Sister Mary Lois at the New York convent.
Hand-done copper enamels with religious themes - *write to* Sister Ellen Stephen at the Vails Gate convent.

Guest and Retreat Facilities
CONVENT OF ST HELENA, VAILS GATE, NEW YORK - Seventeen rooms, no restrictions, cost by donation.
CONVENT OF ST HELENA, AUGUSTA, GEORGIA - Twelve rooms, no restrictions, cost by donation.

Fellowship of Associates
FELLOWSHIP OF ASSOCIATES - open to all women and men. Write to the Fellowship Secretary at the Vails Gate Convent.

Registered Charity Number US Government 501(c)(3) organization.

Sisterhood of the Holy Nativity

SHN

Founded 1882

101 East Division Street
Fond du Lac
WI 54935
USA
Tel: 920 921 2560
E-Mail: shn@vbe.com

St Mary's Retreat Ho.
505 East Los Olivos St.
Santa Barbara
CA 93105
USA
Tel: 805 682 4117

Ours is a mixed life, which means that we combine an apostolic ministry with a contemplative lifestyle. The Rule of the Sisterhood of the Holy Nativity follows the model of the Rule of St Augustine of Hippo. As such, we strive to make the love of God the motive of all our actions. The four 'charisms' which undergird our life are Charity, Humility, Prayer, and Missionary Zeal. Each of these spiritual gifts we desire to develop in our lives both for the fraternal unity they foster among us, and for the power they provide for the work of evangelistic ministry.

Guest and Retreat Facilities
St Mary's Retreat House provides retreats for groups or individuals, with accommodation for twenty-six. It is located near beautiful beaches in California. The House is closed on Thursdays.

Associates and Companions
ASSOCIATES are men and women who connect themselves to the prayer life and ministry of the community, and keep a Rule of Life. Membership is open to adult (lay and clerical) members of the Episcopal Church.
COMPANIONS are young people between the ages of twelve and eighteen who are members of the Episcopal Church and who keep a Rule of Life.

Sisterhood of the Epiphany

SE

Founded 1902

All Hallows Convent
Ditchingham
Bungay
Suffolk
NR35 2DT
UK

Tel: 01986 892749

Lauds
6.40 am
(7.30 am Sat & Sun)

Eucharist
7.15 am (9.30 am Sat, 10.00 am Sun)

Terce
9.30 am (weekdays only)

Sext
12 noon

None
2.00 pm

Evening Prayer
5.30 pm

Compline
8.45 pm

Office Book:
Daily Prayer; Book of Common Prayer & Alternative Service Book Evensong on a regular basis.

Founded for work in India as the Oxford Mission Sisterhood of the Epiphany, the sisters are now based at Ditchingham with the Community of All Hallows. The Christa Sevika Sangha (see separate entry, page 35), founded in 1970, which works in Barisal and Jobarpar, Bangladesh, was under the guidance of the Sisterhood of the Epiphany for some years.

MOTHER WINIFRED SE
(Revd Mother, assumed office 6 January 1997)
Sister Joan
Sister Florence
Sister Rosamund

Community Publication
The Oxford Mission News, twice a year.
Write to Oxford Mission, PO Box 86, Romsey, Hampshire SO51 8YD *Tel: 01794 515004.*
Annual subscription costs £4, post free.

Community History
Brethren of the Epiphany, *A Hundred Years in Bengal,* ISPCK, Delhi, 1979

Fellowship of the Epiphany
The Oxford Mission Fellowship of the Epiphany was founded in 1921 for friends of the Mission in India, Bangladesh, the British Isles and elsewhere.
Current membership:
India: 42; Bangladesh: 25; British Isles: 39; elsewhere: 3.

Sisterhood of St John the Divine

SSJD

Founded 1884

St John's Convent
1 Botham Road
Toronto
Ontario M2N 2J5
CANADA
Tel: 416 226 2201
Fax: 416 222 4442
E-Mail:
ssjd.convent@ecunet.org

Morning Prayer
8.30 am (7.15 am Sun)

Holy Eucharist
12 noon (8.00 am Sun; no Eucharist on Wed)

Noon Office
12.30 pm (Sun only)

Evening Prayer
5.00 pm (7.00 pm Sat)

Compline
8.10 pm (Mon to Thu)

The timetable is subject to variation.

Office Book:
Book of Alternative Services 1985

Registered Charity:
No. BN 11925 4266 RR001 (Canada)

The Sisterhood of St John the Divine is a prayer- and Gospel-centered monastic community, nurtured by our founding vision, open and responsive to the needs of the Church and the contemporary world, continually asking the guidance of the Holy Spirit. We are bound together by the call to live out our baptismal covenant in community.

The traditional religious vows of poverty, chastity and obedience are the way we have chosen to live into our baptism. Living as we do in a time of immense change, the vows anchor us in the life of Jesus, and in the transforming experience of the Gospel. An emphasis on corporateness is one of the strengths of SSJD. The important decisions which affect our lives are made through Chapter meetings and Community Days.

We are committed to a balance of life in which prayer, work, rest, study and recreation each has its place, and in living with the tensions involved in seeking this balance. Meditation, spiritual reading and prayerful reading of the scriptures is at the heart of our daily life, and everything else that we do grows out of it. The work we do may involve sharing our many gifts through pastoral ministries, spiritual direction, making hand-made altar linens, work with Associates, membership on committees at both national and diocesan levels, ordained ministry, writing books and poetry, social justice concerns, composing hymns and music, liturgical reform, creative expression in art, or providing retreats and hospitality.

Addresses of other Houses in Canada

St John's Rehabilitation Hospital,
285 Cummer Avenue, North York, Ontario M2M 2G1
Tel: 416 226 6780; Fax: 416 226 6265
E-Mail: SSJD_Hospital&@ecunet.org
This is a public hospital providing speciality rehabilitation and patient-focussed programs.

St John's Priory,
11717-93 Street, Edmonton, Alberta T5G 1E2
Tel: 403 780 7456; Fax: 403 780 6280
E-Mail: SSJD_Priory@ecunet.org
This has a guest wing, retreats and serves Associates in the West.

St John's House/Maison St Jean,
840 Notre Dame Avenue, St Lambert, Quebec J4R 1R8
Tel: 450 671 5898; Fax: 450 671 5996
Opened in 1998, this has facilities for guests, Associates in the East, missions and retreats.

SISTER CONSTANCE JOANNA SSJD
(*Revd Mother, assumed office 9 May 1994, re-installed 5 May 1999*)
SISTER THELMA-ANNE SSJD (*Assistant to the Revd Mother*)

Sister Constance
Sister Barbara
Sister Nora
Sister Joyce
Sister Helena
Sister Rosemary Anne (*priest*)
Sister Mary Esther
Sister Marilyn
Sister Philippa
Sister Margaret Ann
Sister Wilma
Sister Frances Joyce
Sister Teresa
Sister Jean
Sister Beryl
Sister Merle
Sister Doreen
Sister Rebekah
Sister Patricia
Sister Madeleine Mary
Sister Jocelyn
Sister Margaret Ruth
Sister Sarah Jean
Sister Anitra
Sister Janis Mary
Sister Margaret Mary
Sister Jessica
Sister Elizabeth Ann
Sister Valerie
Sister Brenda
Sister Elaine
Sister Anne

Novices: 4

Obituaries
20 May 1998 Sister Sharon, aged 66, professed 10 years
4 August 1998 Sister Faith, aged 98, professed 65 years

Community Publication
The Eagle (newsletter). Contact the Convent Secretary. Published quarterly. $5.00 annually; subscriptions due in May.

Community History
Sister Eleonora SSJD, *A Memoir of the Life of and Work of Hannah Grier Coombe, Mother-Foundress of the Sisterhood of St John the Divine, Toronto, Canada,* OUP, London, 1933 (out of print).
The Sisterhood of St John the Divine 1884-1984, published 1931 as *A Brief History;* 4th revision 1984, available at the Convent for $4.00.

Community Wares
Wings - a book of poems by Sisters; *Songs for Celebration* - music and words by Sisters Thelma-Anne & Rosemary Anne; T-shirts and sweatshirts with SSJD Logo; printed cards calligraphed by Sisters; cards with photo taken by Sisters. Good selection of books on spiritual growth - not SSJD. All for sale at the Convent (but not by mail).

Guest and Retreat Facilities
Guest Wing with nineteen rooms (twenty-one people) used for rest, quiet time and

retreats. Contact the Guest Sister at the Convent for details about scheduled group retreats - most are given by sisters. Contact the Mission Sister at the Convent for details.

The houses in Edmonton and Montreal also take guests and conduct retreats - contact these houses for detailed information.

Associates

Our approximately nine hundred associates are women and men who follow a Rule of Life and share in the ministry of the Sisterhood. The Sisterhood of St John the Divine owes its founding to the vision and dedication of some women and men many of whom became the first Associates of SSJD. A year of discernment is required before being admitted as an Associate to see if the Associate Rule helps the person in what she/he is seeking; a year which is a time for developing a relationship with the Sisters and deepening the understanding and practice of prayer. The Associate's Rule provides a framework for the journey of faith. There are three basic commitments: belonging in a parish; the practice of retreat and reading of scripture; and the relationship with SSJD. Write to the Sister in the SSJD house nearest to you for further information.

Sisters of St John the Divine, with friends, at the blessing of their new branch house and chapel in St Lambert, Quebec, on 25 March 1999

Sisters of Charity

SC

Founded 1869

St Elizabeth's House
Longbrook Road
Plympton St Maurice
Plymouth
PL7 1NL
UK

Tel: 01752 336112

Morning Prayer
7.00 am

Holy Eucharist
8.00 am

Midday Office
12.00 noon

Vespers
5.00 pm

Compline
9.00 pm

Office Book:
Daily Prayer

Registered Charity:
No. X33170

A Community following the Rule of St Vincent de Paul and so committed to the service of those in need. Retreatants and guests are welcomed at the Mother House. The Sisters are involved in parish and mission work, chiefly in the Plymouth area, and they have a Mission House in Sunderland. The Community also has a nursing home in Plympton and a retreat house in Nevada in the USA.

MOTHER MARY THERESA SC
(Revd Mother, assumed office 6 June 1987)
SISTER ELIZABETH MARY SC (*Assistant)*

Sister Rosalie
Sister Joan Vincent
Sister Faith Mary
Sister Theresa
Sister Angela Mary
Sister Rosamund
Sister Hilda Mary
Sister Faith Nicolette
Sister Philippa Margaret
Sister Margaret Veronica
Sister Mary Joseph
Sister Gabriel Margaret
Sister Clare *(priest)*
Sister Mary Patrick
Sister Julian Hope
Sister Mary Martha
Novices: 1

Obituaries

1 May 1999 Sister Muriel, aged 88, professed 64 years

Other addresses

6 North View, Castletown, Sunderland SR5 3AF, UK.

Convent & Retreat Centre, 701 Park Place, PO Box 60818, Boulder City, Nevada 89006, USA. *Tel: 702 293 4988*

Guest and Retreat Facilities

ST ELIZABETH'S HOUSE There is limited accommodation for retreatants. Two or three conducted retreats are held each year. Parish Groups and other organisations may use the facilities for Quiet Days. We also welcome individuals for private retreats and Quiet Days.

Most convenient time to telephone: 4.00 pm - 8.30 pm

Oblates and Associates

The Community has a group of Oblates, associates and Friends, formed as a mutual supportive link. We do not provide a rule of life; instead we ask our Oblates and associates to add to their existing rule the daily use of the Community Prayer and the Holy Paraclete hymn. This hymn has been said three times a day by all Sisters from the beginning of the Community. Oblates are also invited to use one of the Daily Offices, thereby joining in spirit in the Divine Office of the Community. Oblates and Associates are encouraged to make an annual retreat, if possible at one of the Community houses. Friends support us by their prayers and annual subscription.

Sisters of the Incarnation

SI

Founded 1981

The House of the Incarnation
2 Prelate Court
Wynn Vale
SA 5127
AUSTRALIA

TEL: 08 8289 3737

Office Book:
A Prayer Book for Australia (1995 edition) for Morning and Evening Prayer, and Compline; Midday Office is from another source.

The sisters live under vows of poverty, chastity and obedience in a simple life style, and seek to maintain a balance between prayer, community life and work for each member and to worship and serve within the church. They combine the monastic and apostolic aspects of the Religious Life. The monastic aspects include prayer, domestic work at home, community life and hospitality. The sisters are engaged in parish ministry and exercise a Ministry in Spirituality from the House of the Incarnation at Wynn Vale.

The community was founded in the diocese of Adelaide in 1981 as a contemporary expression of the Religious Life for women in the Anglican Church. In 1988, the two original sisters made their Profession of Life Intention within the Sisters of the Incarnation, before the Archbishop of Adelaide, the Visitor of the community. One member was ordained to the diaconate in 1990 and the priesthood in 1993. The governing body of the community is its chapter of professed sisters, which elects the Guardian, and appoints an Episcopal Visitor and a Community Advisor.

The community is not endowed; the sisters work to earn sufficient for their needs.

SISTER PATRICIA SI
(*Guardian, assumed office 1981*)
Sister Juliana (*priest*)

Friends

The community has a group of Friends who share special celebrations and significant events, many of whom have supported the community from the beginning, while others become Friends as we touch their lives. There is no formal structure.

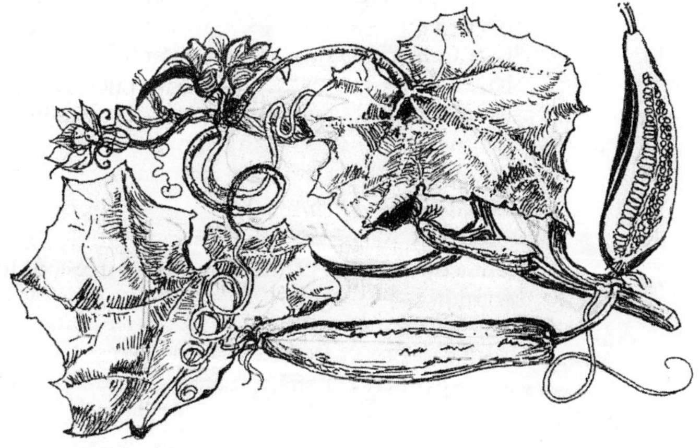

Society of the Holy Cross

SHC

Founded 1925

3 Chong-dong,
Jung-ku,
Seoul 100-120,
KOREA

Tel: 2 735 7832
(& 3478)

Fax: 2 736 5028

E-Mail:
sothc@chollian.net
or
isoh@bule.skhu.ac.kr

The Rt Revd Mark Trollope, the third Bishop of the Anglican Church of Korea founded the Society of the Holy Cross for women and admitted Sister Phoebe Lee as the first postulant. The Sisters of St Peter, of Woking in the UK, who had been missionaries in Korea since 1892, started and nourished this young community. The Sisters live in community with the spirituality of a modified form of the Augustinian Rule. They seek to follow Jesus Christ and they take the three vows of poverty, chastity and obedience.

The Sisters' activities at present include: working in parishes; making wafers, wine and vestments for Holy Communion; running a Retreat and Guest House; running St Bona House for women with learning difficulties and St Anne's Home for elderly women; teaching at St Peter's School for children with learning difficulties; teaching, counselling and being a chaplain at the Anglican University; counselling women's projects in Seoul Diocese, such as writing *A History of Women in the Anglican Church of Korea*, and building a women's center, and giving talks on feminism.

MOTHER EDITH YOUNG JA PARK SHC
(Leader, assumed office 1 Jan 1996)
SISTER CECILIA SHC *(Deputy Leader)*

Sister Tabitha
Sister Maria
Sister Maria Agnes
Sister Esther
Sister Monica
Sister Phoebe Anne
Sister Maria Helen
Sister Etheldreda
Sister Aeun
Sister Catherine
Sister Maria Clare
Sister Pauline
Sister Angela *(Novice Guardian)*
Sister Monica Alma
Sister Martha Joanna
Sister Helena Elizabeth
Sister Theresa
Sister Grace
Sister Lucy Juliana
Sister Anna Frances
Sister Susanna
Sister Lucy Edward
Sister Lucy Jemma

Community Publication

Holy Cross Newsletter, published quarterly (in Korean). Contact the Sisters of the Holy Cross in Seoul for a subscription.

Society of the Precious Blood (Lesotho)

SPB

Founded 1905

Priory of Our Lady Mother of Mercy
PO Box 7192
Maseru 100
LESOTHO

Tel: 36 0217

Morning Prayer
6.15 am

Eucharist
7.00 am

Terce
9.45 am

Midday Office
12 noon

Evening Prayer
5.30 pm

Compline
8.00 pm

Office Book:
Daily Prayer
&
An Anglican Prayer Book (1989)

Five Sisters of the Society of the Precious Blood at Burnham Abbey came to Masite in Lesotho in 1957 to join with a community of African women, with the intention of forming a multi-cultural contemplative community dedicated to intercession. In 1966, this community at Masite became autonomous, although still maintaining strong ties of friendship with Burnham Abbey. In 1980, a House of Prayer was established in Kimberley in South Africa, which has developed a more active branch of the Society.

SISTER ELAINE MARY SPB
(*Prioress, assumed office 24 September 1997*)

Sister Josephine Mary
Sister Theresia Mary
Sister Magdalen Mary
Sister Lucia Mary
Sister Mary Dominic
Sister Diana Mary
Sister Cicily Mary
Sister Camilla Mary

Novices: 1
Intern Oblates: 2

Obituaries
May 1999 Sister Mary Julian

Other House
St Monica's House of Prayer, 46 Green Street, West End, Kimberley, 8301 SOUTH AFRICA

Community Publication
Annual *Newsletter;* apply to the Prioress. No charge.

Community Wares
Christmas cards, handicrafts, religious booklets.

Guest and Retreat Facilities
There is a small guest house with four bedrooms. There is no fixed charge. It is closed in winter (from mid-June to mid-August).

Oblates and Companions
The Community has twelve oblates (in South Africa, Zambia and Zimbabwe), and eighty-five Companions and Associates (in Lesotho and South Africa). All renew their promises annually. Oblates are sent prayer material every six weeks. Companions and Associates receive quarterly letters and attend occasional quiet days.

Society of the Precious Blood (UK)

SPB

Founded 1905

Burnham Abbey
Lake End Road
Taplow
Maidenhead
Berkshire SL6 OPW
UK

Tel & Fax:
01628 604080

St Pega's Hermitage
Peakirk
Peterborough PE6 7NP
UK
Tel: 01733 252219

Lauds
6.00 am (6.15 am Sun)
Matins
7.30 am
Eucharist
9.00 am
Sext
12.00 noon
Vespers
5.30 pm
Compline
8.30 pm

Registered Charity :
No. 900512

We are a contemplative community whose particular work within the whole body of Christ is worship, thanksgiving and intercession. Within these ancient Abbey walls, which date back to 1266, we continue to live the Augustinian monastic tradition of prayer, silence, fellowship and solitude. The Eucharist is the centre of our life, where we find ourselves most deeply united with Christ, one another and all for whom we pray. The work of prayer is continued in the Divine Office, in the Watch before the Blessed Sacrament and in our whole life of work, reading, creating, and learning to live together. This life of prayer finds an outward expression in welcoming guests, who come seeking an opportunity for quiet and reflection in which to deepen their own spiritual lives.

SISTER ELIZABETH MARY SPB
(Revd Mother, assumed office 28 January 1998)
Sisters in Profession: 23 *Novices*: 1

Community Publication
Newsletter, yearly at Christmas. *Companions/Oblates Letter*, quarterly.

Community History
Sister Felicity Mary SPB, *Mother Millicent Mary of the Will of God*, Macmillan, London, 1968.
Booklets and leaflets on the history and life of the Abbey and the Community.

I will most gladly spend and be spent ~ ~ SPB

Community Wares
The Sisters find a creative outlet in producing cards, rosaries, holding crosses and other crafts (for sale in the Guest House).

Guest and Retreat Facilities
We have a small guest house with five single rooms for individual (unconducted) retreats. We also have a cottage with self-catering facilities for retreats and sabbaticals.

Most convenient time to telephone: 10.30 am - 12 noon, 2.30 pm - 4.00 pm.

Companions and Oblates
Companions and Oblates of the Society are Christians who wish to identify themselves with the life and aims of the Society and to share in its worship and intercession as fully as possible according to the varying circumstances of their lives.

The Watch before the Blessed Sacrament, interceding for the whole of creation, is kept throughout the day and for most of the night.

It is the love of God that tears us away from the world, and the same love that links us to one another - if we love God we shall be of one heart and soul together.
Mother Millicent Mary SPB

Society of the Sacred Advent

SSA

Founded 1892

Community House
34 Lapraik Street
Albion
QLD 4010
AUSTRALIA
Tel: 07 3262 5511
Fax: 07 3862 3296

Quiet time
6.00 am

Morning Prayer
6.30 am
(7.00 am Sun & Mon)

Eucharist
7.00 am
(7.30 am Sun, 5.00 pm Mon)

Midday Prayer
12 noon

Evensong
5.30 pm

Compline
7.30 pm
(8.00 pm Wed & Sat)

Office Book:
A Prayer Book for Australia;
The Daily Office SSF is used for Midday Office

The Society of the Sacred Advent exits for the glory of God and for the service of His Church in preparation for the Second Coming of our Lord and Saviour Jesus Christ.

Members devote themselves to God in community under vows of poverty, chastity and obedience. Our life is a round of prayer, silence and work. Our Patron is John the Baptist who, by his life and death, pointed the way to Jesus. We would hope also to point the way to Jesus in our own time, to a world which has largely lost touch with spiritual realities and is caught up in despair, loneliness and fear.

The Society has two schools. However, Sisters no longer have a day-to-day involvement. Two Sisters are on each of the School Councils. St Margaret's School has day and boarding students; St Aidan's has day students only. Both schools are for girls only.

MOTHER EUNICE SSA
(Revd Mother, assumed office 29 September 1982)

Sister Joan Michael*
Sister Dorothy
Sister Joyce Mary*
Sister June Ruth
Sister Sandra
Sister Beverley
Sister Gillian

Novices: 1

*St Martin's Nursing Home

Community Publication
There is a Newsletter, twice yearly. For a subscription, write to Sister Sandra SSA . The cost is A$5 per year.

Community History
Elizabeth Moores, *One Hundred Years of Ministry,* published for SSA, 1992.

Community Wares
Cards and crafts.

Guest and Retreat Facilities

There are twenty single rooms. Both men and women are welcome. The facilities are closed over Christmas and in January.

As part of this ministry, Sisters may be called to give addresses, conduct Retreats or Quiet Days, or make themselves available for individual spiritual direction. The aim of the Community is to grow in the mind of Christ so as to manifest Him to others.

Fellowship and Company

THE FELLOWSHIP OF THE SACRED ADVENT Since 1925, the work of the Community has been helped by the prayers and work of a group of friends known as the Fellowship of the Sacred Advent. They have a simple Rule of Life.

THE COMPANY OF THE SACRED ADVENT began in 1987. This is a group of men and women, clergy and lay, bound together in love for Jesus Christ and His Church in the spirit of St John the Baptist. It seeks to proclaim the Advent challenge: 'Prepare the Way of the Lord.' Members have a Rule of Life and renew their promises annually.

Members of the Fellowship and Company are part of our extended Community family. The Sisters arrange Retreats and Quiet Days and support them with their prayers, help, or spiritual guidance, as required.

Society of the Sacred Cross

SSC

Founded 1914 (Chichester); re-established in 1923 (Wales)

*Tymawr Convent
Lydart
Monmouth
Gwent
NP25 4RN
UK
Tel: 01600 860244*

Morning Prayer
7.00 am

Terce
8.45 am

Eucharist
12.00 noon

Evening Prayer
5.30 pm

Compline
8.30 pm

Office Book: Celebrating Common Prayer, with additional SSC material

Registered Charity: No. 1047614

The community, part of the Anglican Church in Wales, lives a monastic, contemplative life of prayer based on silence, solitude and learning to live together, under vows of poverty, chastity and obedience, with a modern rule, Cistercian in spirit. At the heart of our corporate life is the Eucharist with the daily Office and other times of shared prayer spanning the day. All services are open to the public and we are often joined by members of the neighbourhood in addition to our visitors. Our common life includes study, recreation and work in the house and extensive grounds. It is possible for women and men, married or single, to experience our life of prayer by living alongside the community for periods longer than the usual guest stay. Hospitality is an important part of our life at Tymawr and guests are most welcome. We also organise and sponsor occasional lectures and programmes of study for those who wish to find or develop the life of the spirit in their own circumstances. The community is dedicated to the crucified and risen Lord as the focus of its life and the source of the power to live it.

SISTER MARY JEAN SSC
(Revd Mother, assumed office 2 July 1998)
SISTER ANNE SSC *(Assistant)*

Sister Jeanne
Sister Clare
Sister Rosemary
Sister Paula
Sister Veronica Ann
Sister Lorna Francis*
Sister Heylin Columba*

Sister Mary Janet
Sister Gillian Mary
Sister Susan
Sister Cara Mary
Sister Joan

Novices: 1

* *Living the contemplative life away from Tymawr.*

Community Publication

Tymawr Newsletter, yearly at Advent. Write to the above address.

Guest and Retreat Facilities

The community offers facilities for individual guests and small groups. There are five rooms (one double) in the guest wing of the Main House for full board. Michaelgarth, the self-catering guest house, offers facilities for individuals or groups (five singles and two doubles). Individuals may have private retreats with guidance from a member of the community. The community occasionally organises retreat and quiet days. Please write with a stamped addressed envelope for details.

Most convenient time for guests to telephone:
6.45 pm – 8.00 pm only, except Fridays and Sundays.

Oblates and Associates
There are thirty-eight Oblates, living in their own homes, each having a personal Rule sustaining their life of prayer. Four Companion brothers and a Companion group meet regularly at Tymawr under a Rule appropriate to their ministries and life. There are sixty-three Women Associates and fifty Men Associates with a simple commitment, who are part of the extended family.

Tymawr Convent

Society of the Sacred Mission

SSM

Founded 1893

Founded in 1893 by Father Herbert Kelly, the Society is a means of uniting the devotion of ordinary people, using it in the service of the Church. Members of the Society share a common life of prayer and fellowship in a variety of educational, pastoral and community activities in England, Australia, Japan, Lesotho, Papua New Guinea and South Africa.

CHRISTOPHER MYERS SSM
(*Director, assumed office August 1996*)
DOUGLAS BROWN SSM
(*Provincial for the Northern Province, assumed office April 1998*)

Paul Hume
Alban Perkins
Clement Mullenger
Laurence Eyers
John Lewis
Austin Masters
Frank Green
Anthony Perry
Henry Arkell
Hilary Greenwood
Andrew Longley
David Wells
Gordon Holroyd
Francis Horner
Dunstan McKee
Ralph Martin
Thomas Brown
Andrew Muramatsu
Jonathan Ewer
Rodney Hart
Edmund Wheat
Michael Lapsley
Matthew Dowsey
Colin Griffiths
William Nkomo
Robert Stretton
Roderick McDougall
Steven Haws
Steven de Kleer

Novices, Southern Province: 4

Obituaries

27 Feb 1998 Brother Peter Story, aged 63 years, professed 36 years

Community Publication

Sacred Mission (newsletter of the Southern Province): The Editor, St James' House, Wollaston College, Mount Claremont, Perth, Western Australia 6010

SSM News (newsletter of the Northern Province): The Secretary, SSM Newsletter, St Antony's Priory, Claypath, Durham DH1 1QT, UK

Office Book: Celebrating Common Prayer

Community History

Herbert H Kelly SSM, *A Idea in the Working,* SSM Press, Kelham, 1908

Alistair Mason, *SSM: History of the Society of the Sacred Mission*, Canterbury Press, Norwich, 1993.

Addresses

NORTHERN PROVINCE

St Antony's Priory
Claypath
Durham
DH1 1QT
UK
Tel: 0191 384 3747
Fax: 0191 384 4939

1 Linford Lane
Milton Keynes
Bucks
MK15 9DL
UK
Tel: 01908 663749

House of the Sacred Mission
90 Vassall Road
London
SW9 6JA
UK
Tel: 0207 582 2040
Fax: 0207 582 6640

House of the Sacred Mission, Vassall Road

SOUTHERN PROVINCE

St John's Priory
14 St John's Street
Adelaide
SOUTH AUSTRALIA 5000
Tel: 08 8223 1014
Fax: 08 8223 2764

St Michael's Priory
75 Watson's Road
Diggers Rest
Victoria 3427
AUSTRALIA
Tel: 03 9740 1618
Fax: 03 9740 0007

Newton Theological College
PO Box 162
Popondetta
Ora Province
PAPUA NEW GUINEA

Priory of the Sacred Mission
PO Box 1579
Maseru 100
LESOTHO

Companions and Associates

COMPANIONS: are men and women who support the aims of the Society without being closely related to any of its work. The Companions consecrate their lives in loving response to a vocation to deepen their understanding of God's will, and to persevere more devotedly in commitments already made - in baptism, marriage or ordination.

ASSOCIATES: are those who support the Aims of the Society, and actively share in its work.

Society of St Francis

SSF

Founded 1919 (USA) 1921 (UK)

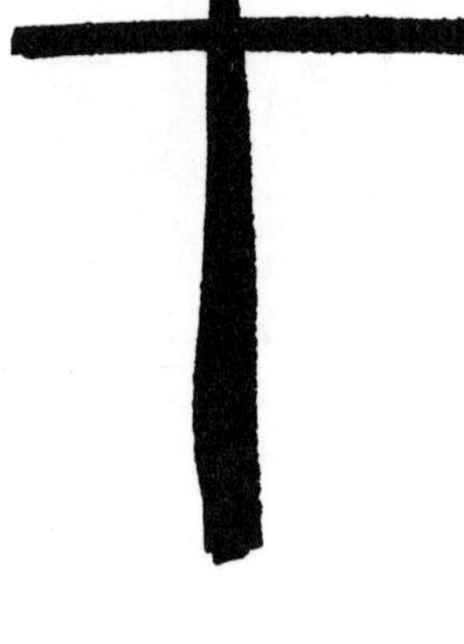

Office Book: The Daily Office SSF

European Province SSF Registered Charity: No. 236464

European Province Website: http://www.orders.anglican.org/ssf/

The Society of St Francis has diverse origins in a number of Franciscan groups which drew together during the 1930s to found one Franciscan Society. SSF in its widest definition includes First Order Brothers, First Order Sisters (CSF), Second Order Sisters (OSC) and a Third Order. The First Order shares a common life of prayer, fraternity and a commitment to the poor. In its larger houses, this includes accommodation for short-term guests; in the city houses, the Brothers are engaged in a variety of ministries, chaplaincies and care for poor people. The Brothers are also available for retreat work, for counselling and for sharing in the task of mission in parishes and schools. They also undertake work in Europe and there are houses in America, Australasia and the Pacific.

DANIEL SSF
(Minister General, assumed office 1 July 1997)

EUROPEAN PROVINCE

DAMIAN SSF
(Minister Provincial, assumed office 1 July 1991)
SAMUEL SSF *(Assistant Minister)*

Aidan
Alan Michael
Alistair
Amos
Angelo
Anselm
Arnold
Austin
Benedict
Benjamin
Bernard
Christian
David
David Francis
David Jardine
David Stephen
Desmond Alban
Dominic Christopher
Donald
Edmund
Edward
Geoffrey
Giles
Gordon
Gregory
Harry
Hubert
Hugo
James Anthony
James Edward
James William
Jason
John Francis
Jonathan
Julian
Kentigern John
Kevin
Malcolm
Martin
Matthew
Michael
Nathanael
Nicholas Alan
Nolan Tobias
Paschal
Paul
Paul Anthony
Peter Douglas

Philip	Robert Coombes	Tristam
Philip Bartholomew	Roger Alexander	Vincent
Ramon	Ronald	Wilfrid
Raphael	Seraphim	
Raymond Christian	Simeon Christopher	*Novices:* 6
Reginald	Thomas Anthony	

Obituaries

24 Oct 1998 Robbie Asaph, aged 44, professed 5 years

Addresses

The Friary
Alnmouth, Alnwick
Northumberland NE66 3NJ
Tel: 01665 830213 or 01665 830660
Fax: 01665 830580
E-Mail: Alnmouthfr@aol.com

St Clare House
34 Claerwen Grove
Birmingham B31 1TY
Tel: 0121 475 4482

Saint Francis House
14/15 Botolph Lane
Cambridge CB2 3RD
Tel: 01223 353903 or 01223 321576

The Little Portion
111/2 Lothian Road
Edinburgh EH3 9AN
Tel: 0131 228 3077

(*Minister Provincial*)
Alverna , 110 Ellesmere Road
Gladstone Park
London NW10 1JS
Tel: 0208 452 7285
Fax: 0208 452 1946
E-Mail: Damianssf@aol.com

16 Dalserf Street
Barrowfield
Glasgow G31 4AS
Tel: 0141 550 1202

St Mary-at-the-Cross
Glasshampton
Shrawley
Worcestershire WR6 6TQ
Tel: 01299 896345
Fax: 01299 896083

The Friary of St Francis
Hilfield
Dorchester
Dorset DT2 7BE
Tel: 01300 341345
Fax: 01300 341293
E-Mail: HilfieldUK@ssf.orders.anglican.org

Holy Trinity House
Orsett Terrace
Paddington
London W2 6AH
Tel: 0207 723 9735

House of the Divine Compassion
42 Balaam Street
Plaistow
London E13 8AQ
Tel: 0207 476 5189

10 Halcrow Street
Stepney
London E1 2EP
Tel: 0207 247 6233

Community History

Petà Dunstan, *This Poor Sort: A History of the European Province of the Society of Saint Francis*, DLT, 1997, £19.95 + £2 p&p.

Community Wares
Hilfield Friary shop has friary-made prayer stools, 'Freeland' cards & traidcraft goods.

Community Publications
franciscan, three times a year, for which an annual subscription is £4.50. Write to the Subscriptions Secretary at Hilfield Friary.
Books available from Hilfield Friary book shop include:
The Daily Office SSF: A version of Celebrating Common Prayer, £10.00 + £2 p&p.

Guest and Retreat Facilities
ALNMOUTH The Friary has twelve rooms (including one twin-bedded) for men or women guests. Some conducted retreats are held each year and individually-guided retreats are available on request.
GLASSHAMPTON The guest accommodation, available to both men and women, comprises five rooms. Groups can visit for the day, but may not exceed fifteen people.
HILFIELD The Guest House, for men and women guests, was refurbished early in 1998 and contains eleven single rooms plus a double room which has wheelchair access. The friary is closed Mondays, so guests may stay from Tuesday to Sunday afternoon.

Companions
Companions are individual Christians who wish to associate themselves with the Society through prayer, friendship and in seeking to live the spirit of the Gospel in the way of St Francis. For more information about becoming a Companion contact: The Secretary for Companions, Hilfield Friary, Dorchester, Dorset DT2 7BE, UK.

AUSTRALIA/NEW ZEALAND PROVINCE

SSF friars went from England to Papua New Guinea in the late 1950s and the first Australian house was established in 1964. The first New Zealand house followed in 1970. In 1981, the Pacific Province was divided into two: Australia/New Zealand and the Pacific Islands.

COLIN WILFRED SSF
(Minister Provincial, assumed office 1 July 1997)

Alfred Boonkong
Andrew Philip
Brian
Bruce-Paul
Christopher John
Damian Kenneth
Donald Campbell
Francis
Leo Anthony
Masseo
Noel-Thomas
Peter-Christian
William

Novices: 2

Office Book
The Daily Office SSF. At the Auckland friary, this is used with New Zealand adaptations.

Addresses

The Hermitage
PO Box 46
Stroud
NSW 2425
AUSTRALIA
Tel: 2 4994 5372
Fax: 2 4994 5527
E-Mail:
ssfstrd@midac.com.au

The Friary
115 Cornwall St
Annerley
Brisbane
QD 4103
AUSTRALIA
Tel: 7 3391 3915
Fax: 7 3391 3916

St Francis Friary
PO Box 89-085
Torbay
Auckland
AOTEAROA/NEW ZEALAND
Tel: 9 473 2605
Fax: 9 473 2606
E-Mail:
ssfauckland@xtra.co.nz

Community Publication

Franciscan Angles, published three times a year. To be put on the mailing list, write to the Auckland address. Subscription is by donation.

Guest and Retreat facilities

There is limited accommodation for short stay guests available in the Brisbane and Auckland friaries, and the Hermitage at Stroud. Payment is by donation.

Community Wares

Booklets, cards and candles are available from the Hermitage at Stroud.

PACIFIC ISLANDS PROVINCE

Papua New Guinea Region

CLIFTON HENRY SSF
(*Regional Minister, Papua New Guinea Region*)

Ananias Korina
Andrew
Anthony
Benjamin Tapio
Benstead Ponoba
Bray Ungaia
Cecil Okun
Charles Iada
Daniel Gorua
Gilson Kira
Hugh
Laurence Hauje
Leonard Richardson
Lester
Lester Meso
Mishael Eruga
Moses Vavakadiba
Nathanael Gari
Oswald
Peter Kevin
Philip Etobae
Ronald Goviro
Selwyn Suma
Smith Tovebae
Timothy Joseph
Walter

Novices: 9

Addresses

St Mary of the Angels Friary
Haruro, PO Box 78
Popondetta 241
Oro Province
PAPUA NEW GUINEA

Dipoturu
PO Box 78
Popondetta 241
Oro Province
PAPUA NEW GUINEA

Katerada
PO Box 78
Popondetta 241
Oro Province
PAPUA NEW GUINEA

Douglas House
PO Box 3411
Lae
Morobe Province
PAPUA NEW GUINEA
Tel & fax: 472 1842

Siomoromoro Friary
PO Box 1323
Goroka
Eastern Highlands Province
PAPUA NEW GUINEA

The Friary
PO Box 19
Dogura
Milne Bay Province
PAPUA NEW GUINEA

Pacific Islands Province

Solomons Islands Region

Andrew Manu SSF
(*Regional Minister, Solomon Islands Region*)

Alen Lafumana
Ashley Vaisu
Athanasius
Bartholomew Maesiwou
Colin
Comins Romano
Davidson Warismae
Dudley Palmer
Gabriel Maelesi
George Huinodi
Godfrey Kemangava
Layban Kwanafia
Manasseh Birahu
Martin Tauwea
Moses Lonsdale
Nicholas Tai
Patteson Kwa'ai
Peter Abuofa
Robert Briel
Samson Amoni
Samson Siho
Shadrack Mamaone
Shedrick Iru
Stanley Sinewala
Wilson Bosa
Winston Paoni

Novices: 16

Addresses

Patteson House
PO Box 519
Honiara
Solomon Islands
Tel: 22386
Regional Office tel & fax: 25810
E-Mail: Francis@welkam.solomon.com.sb

La Verna Friary
Hautambu
PO Box 519
Honiara
Solomon Islands

Little Portion Friary
Hautambu
PO Box 519
Honiara
Solomon Islands

The Friary
PO Box 7
Auki
Malaita Province
Solomon Islands

San Damiano Friary
Diocese of Hanuato'o
Kira Kira
Makira Ulawa Province
Solomon Islands

Holy Martyrs Friary
Luisalo Training Centre
Santa Cruz
Temotu Province
Solomon Islands

SSF Brothers
St Dominic's RTC
Vanga Point
Gizo
Western Province
Solomon Islands

American Province

The American Province of SSF was founded as the Order of St Francis in 1919 by Father Claude Crookston, who took the name Father Joseph. Under his leadership the community developed, based first in Wisconsin and then on Long Island, New York. The Order originally combined a monastic spirituality with a commitment to missions and evangelizing. Father Joseph also founded a community of enclosed sisters, the Poor Clares of Reparation. In 1967, the OSF friars amalgamated with the Society of St Francis in the UK and became the American Province of SSF.

Our lives are structured around our times together of formal prayer and the Eucharist, which give our lives a focus. Brothers engage in a wide variety of ministries: community organizing, missions, work in parishes and institutions, counselling and spiritual direction, study, the arts, serving the sick and infirm and people with AIDS. We come from a wide variety of backgrounds and cultural traditions. Living with each other can be difficult, but we work hard to find common ground and to communicate honestly with each other. God takes our imperfections and, in the mystery of Christ's body, makes us whole.

JUSTUS SSF
(*Minister Provincial , assumed office May 1993*)
DEREK SSF (*Assistant Minister*)

Anthony Michael	Jason Robert	Robert Hugh
Antonio Sato	John George	Thomas
Clark Berge	Jon Bankert	
Dunstan	Jude	*Novices:* 1

Order of Poor Clares of Reparation:
Sister Mary Dorothea PCR

Addresses

Little Portion Friary
PO Box 399
Mount Sinai
NY 11766/0399
USA
Tel: 516 473 0533
Fax: 516 473 9434
E-Mail: clarkssf@aol.com

San Damiano
573 Dolores Street
San Francisco
CA 94110
USA
Tel: 415 861 1372
Fax: 415 861 7952
E-Mail: brojude@aol.com

St Elizabeth's Friary
1474 Bushwick Avenue
Brooklyn
NY 11207
USA
Tel: 718 455 5963
Fax: 718 443 3437
E-Mail: derekssf@aol.ssf

Minister Provincial:
Tel & fax: 718 602 2973
E-Mail: justus@societystfrancis.org

Office Book:
Book of Common Prayer of the Episcopal Church of the USA and the CSF Office Book.

Community Publication
The Little Chronicle. Four times a year.

Guest and Retreat Facilities
There is a guest house at Little Portion Friary (Mount Sinai address), with twelve rooms, accommodating a maximum of sixteen guests. It is closed on Mondays. If there is no answer when telephoning, please leave a message on the answering machine.

American Province Website: http://www.societystfrancis.org

Third Order SSF

The Third Order of the Society of St Francis consists of men and women, ordained and lay, married or single, who believe that God is calling them to live out their Franciscan vocation in the world, living in their own homes and doing their own jobs. Living under a rule of life, with the help of a spiritual director, members (called tertiaries) encourage one another in living and witnessing to Christ, being organised in local groups to enable regular meetings to be held. It is international in scope, with a Minister General and five Ministers Provincial to cover the relevant Provinces, as indicated below:

Minister General
The Revd Alden Whitney, MD
Brookside Farm, 167 Long Ridge Road, Danbury, CT 06810,
USA

Minister Provincial, African Province
Mrs Anne Kotze
7 Forest Avenue, Oranjezicht, Cape Town 8001,
South Africa

Minister Provincial, American Province
Mrs Anita Catron
3280 Bernada Drive, Salt Lake City, UT 84124,
USA

Minister Provincial, Australian Province
The Ven. Keith Slater
St Clement's on the Hill, Eudunda Street, Stafford,
Qld 4053,
Australia

Minister Provincial, European Province
Mrs Carolin Clapperton
Lochside, Lochwinnoch, Renfrewshire, PA12 4JH,
UK

(*European Province, Registered Charity Number : 1064356*)

Minister Provincial, New Zealand Province
Revd Dorothy Brooker
38 Rutland Street, Rotorua,
New Zealand

Society of St John the Divine

SSJD

Founded 1887

St John's House
43 Florida Road
Greyville
Durban 4001
SOUTH AFRICA
Tel: 031 234001

Angelus
6.15 am

Mass
6.40 am

Morning Prayer
8.45 am

Midday Office & Angelus
12.15 pm

Evening Office & Angelus
5.00 pm

Compline
8.30 pm

Office Book:
An Anglican Prayer Book 1989 (South African) for Mass, Morning & Evening Prayer; SSJD book for Midday Office & Compline.

The Society has never been a large community, with just sixty professions over a century, and has always worked in Natal. Originally the community ran schools and orphanages, but handed the last of its institutions to the diocese in 1968, and moved from Pietermaritzburg to Durban. The Sisters still have a presence on the Board of St John's Diocesan School and St Martin's Home for Children. For a time after 1968, the Sisters were involved in parish work, and then in retreat work. In 1994, after the death of the older Sisters, the four remaining moved to the present house, which is more central.

Mother Margaret Anne and Sister Mary Evelyn are lay ministers, licensed to preach in any parish of the diocese. In our own parish, Sister Mary Evelyn takes sick communions, and is involved at the hospice and with AIDS patients. Sister Sophia visits a hospice for homeless women and Sister Hilary keeps in touch with St John's School, where she was once a pupil. Mother Margaret Anne is a member of the Diocesan Synod.

MOTHER MARGARET ANNE SSJD
(*Revd Mother, assumed office May 1994*)
Sister Mary Evelyn
Sister Sophia
Sister Hilary

Community Publication
There are two newsletters a year, sent out in May and November. Contact the Revd Mother. There is no charge - donations to cover the cost are made by our Associates and Friends.

Community History
Sister Margaret Anne SSJD, *What the World Counts Weakness*, privately published 1987. Available from St John's House, Durban, price R10.00.

Community Wares
Crocheted girdles for clergy and lay ministers.
Re-conditioned cards.

Guest and Retreat Facilities
There is a small cottage in the grounds comprising two single rooms, both having en suite shower, toilet and handbasin, small kitchenette for making hot drinks, with bar fridge and washing-up facilities. Meals are sent up from the main kitchen. There is a swimming pool avail-

able. The cost is R30-R50 per day. The cottage is closed at Christmas.

Mother Margaret Anne is available by arrangement to guide individually directed retreats (only the cost of accommodation is charged), and the Community organise (advertised) Quiet Days in Lent, and at other times if requested.

Oblates and Associates

OBLATES There are two (non-resident). They have their own Rule of Life, approved by Revd Mother and their spiritual director,and renew their promises annually.

ASSOCIATES There are about 140, some overseas, who have a simple Rule of Life, which is the same for all, and they also renew their promises annually.

FRIENDS There are about 125, some overseas, who pray for the community and are invited to our quarterly meetings, as are the Oblates and Associates.

The Sisters SSJD: back row, left to right: Mother Margaret Anne, Sister Hilary, Sister Mary Evelyn. Front row: Sister Sophia. On the right is the Bishop Visitor to the Sisters, Rt Revd Michael Nuttall.

Society of St John the Evangelist

(North American Congregation)

SSJE

Founded 1866

*980 Memorial Drive
Cambridge
MA 02138-5717
USA*

*Tel: 617 876 3037
Fax: 617 876 5210*

Morning Prayer
6.00 am

Eucharist
7.45 am

Midday Prayer
12.30 pm

Evening Prayer
6.00 pm

Compline
9.00 pm

*Office Book:
Book of Common Prayer of the Episcopal Church of the USA*

The Society of St John the Evangelist is the oldest Religious community for men in the Anglican Communion. The presence of the Society in North America dates from 1871. The community unites men from the USA, Canada and the UK, ordained and lay, in an ordered life of prayer, worship and service. We take vows of poverty, celibacy and obedience, and have developed a modern Rule of Life which was adopted in 1997.

The community has a ministry of hospitality in the city based on the monastery in Cambridge, and in the country at Emery House, West Newbury. We also operate *Cowley Publications,* which publishes religious books for an international Anglican and ecumenical readership, and run the bookstore at the headquarters of the diocese of Massachusetts in Boston.

We serve children and their families in Boston through St. Augustine Ministries, a year-round program providing oversight of the educational, social and spiritual needs of urban children-at-risk. Summer camping is offered to these children at our campus in Foxborough, MA. Brothers pursue other ministries according to their gifts, particularly in spiritual direction, retreat leading, the teaching of prayer. Several brothers work in local hospitals, soup kitchens, prisons and groups meeting the needs of people with HIV/AIDS.

BROTHER MARTIN SMITH SSJE
(*Superior, assumed office June 1992*)
BROTHER JAMES KOESTER SSJE (*Senior Brother*)

Paul Wessinger
David Allen
John Oyama
Bernard Russell
Brian Bostwick
M. Thomas Shaw
Russell Page
John Goldring
Jonathan Maury

Eldridge Pendleton
Curtis Almquist
John Mathis
Brian Willmer
David Vryhof
Michael North
Matthew Holsti

Novices: 4 *Postulants:* 1

Obituaries

30 Apr 1998 Brother Robert Cheney Smith, aged 85, professed 55 years

23 Apr 1999 Brother Robert Greenfield, aged 75, professed 12 years

Other house

Emery House, Emery Lane, West Newbury, MA 01985
Tel: 978 462 7940; Fax: 978 462 0285

Community Publication
Cowley: for a subscription, write to SSJE at the Cambridge, Mass., address. The suggested donation is $15.

Community Wares
Books published by *Cowley Publications* are obtainable from:
Cowley Publications & Cowley Cathedral Book Store,
28 Temple Place, Boston, MA 02111, USA
Bookstore *Tel: 617 423 4719*
Publications *Tel: 617 423 2427* *Fax: 617 423 2354*
E-Mail: cowley@cowley.org
Website: http://www.cowley.org
They are obtainable in the UK & Europe through:
Columba Book Services, 55a Spruce Avenue, Stillorgan Industrial Park,
Black Rock, Dublin, REPUBLIC OF IRELAND. *Tel: 1 294 2560*

Guest and Retreat Facilities
CAMBRIDGE Sixteen rooms. $50 per night. Closed in September.
WEST NEWBURY Seven hermitages and four rooms. $50 per night.

Associates
Fellowship of St John.

The Chapel of the Monastery in Cambridge, Massachusetts

Society of St John the Evangelist

(UK)

SSJE

Founded 1866

St Edward's House
22 Great College Street
Westminster
London
SW1P 3QA
UK

Tel: 020 7 222 9234
Fax: 020 7 799 2641

Mattins
7.00 am

Eucharist
7.30 am
(8.00 am Sun)

Terce
9.45 am

Sext
12.45 pm

Evensong
6.30 pm

Compline
9.30 pm

The Society of Saint John the Evangelist is now training for the future. Novices are called 'Seeker- associate member', and move on to 'Internal Oblate', these being legally recognised terms within the constitution of S.S.J.E. From here the person enters First Vows after about two years. This has enabled the Community to reorder the period before First Vows to allow presence and voting in Chapter. The active life and activities of these new members enable those things for which the older members have been trained, and are still able to do, to go on without hindrance.

The London house hosts or runs retreats, quiet days, and parish conferences. Various groups make use of the house, such as Julian groups, MP's wives, and Prayer for Africa. Business groups come for discussion and midweek Eucharist. Individuals come for study, quiet, spiritual direction, counselling.

Alongside this in London there is new work and outlook. The Community here is, and will be, firmly based on St Edward's House. But each person is being given still more encouragement to use his own gifts which now include (as above) counselling, spiritual direction; also mission to 'the ageing', liturgics, working for healing; mission to people of local Christian communities, people met in the street, and students, especially those of other nationalities. There is the continuing work with artists and the arts world, and with those with dyslexia and M.E.; and also some abuse counselling. The community tries in these and other ways to seek the will of God for its present and future life, and to discern what the church requires of it. The present new people are highly trained in their own way - a big bonus - and discernment of training for newcomers for the future is still in early stages. Of course, the varied activities based on St Edward's House are nothing, if they are not centred in the daily community worship, and each individual's prayer.

At Oxford the small group continues the round of worship and community life, and the house is available for individuals. Father Bean continues his valuable work on butterflies etc. with a visit to the Pitt Rivers Museum once a week for recataloguing their collections.

Other UK address
SSJE Priory, 228 Iffley Road, Oxford OX4 1SE, UK
Tel: 01865 248116

FATHER JAMES NATERS SSJE
(Superior, assumed office 1991)
FATHER ALAN GRAINGE SSJE *(Assistant Superior)*

Father Herbert Slade
Brother Anselm Chiverton
Father Alan Bean
Father Stuart Lennard
Father David Campbell
Father Peter Palmer
Father Alan Cotgrove

Brother Gerald Perkins
Brother Adrian Tate
Brother James Simon

Internal Oblates
Father Nicholas Wickham
Father Peter Huckle

Community Publication
Newsletter, published monthly, is edited by Graham Johnson. All enquiries to Brother James Simon (*Contacts Officer*).

Guest and Retreat Facilities
ST EDWARD'S HOUSE Three conducted retreats are held each year; and there are Quarterly Quiet Days. Individual retreatants are welcomed and there are also facilities for Quiet Days.

THE OXFORD PRIORY also has a room available for retreatants.

The Fellowship of St John
Following Community discussions and Chapter decisions the present 'Fellowship of Saint John' came into being early in 1998.

Its work is to strengthen the ties between two bodies: the members of the Fellowship (who now number over two hundred) and SSJE (members, oblates and seekers). The Fellowship has its own Logo: an eagle in flight.

The Core Committee is made up of area representatives (elected or nominated) and SSJE representatives. This Committee held its first meeting in September 1998. It elected a Management Group to do the day-to-day running. At the present time copies of its *Newsletter* go out to a total of 650 individuals or groups.

Area Groups are growing each month: Ann Gurney leads the London one, Hilary Knight one in the South. There are also Groups in the East Midlands, and the Potteries. There are other members in the rest of the UK, as well as twenty or so members in Australia, Canada, Germany (twinned mainly with the Ecumenical Community of the Holy Cross), New Zealand (including one Oblate), and South Africa. These are all in direct contact with the Contacts Officer at St Edward's House. Full Lists, as well as area lists are sent out for private intercession.

The Fellowship has its own Manual with Office Book; but the Office Book is also available on its own from St Edward's House, price £1.

There is a leaflet, available from the Contacts Officer, for intending prospective members of the Fellowship.

Society of St Margaret

(Aberdeen)

SSM

Founded 1855
(Aberdeen Convent founded 1864)

St Margaret's Convent
17 Spital
Aberdeen
AB24 3HT
UK
Tel: 01224 632648

Office Book:
SSM Office

Registered Charity:
No. 006216 (Scotland)

Saint Margaret's Convent, Aberdeen, is one of the autonomous Houses which constitute the Society of St Margaret, founded by John Mason Neale. The Community is at present engaged in hospital chaplaincy, pastoral and retreat work, and has limited holiday accommodation.

MOTHER VERITY MARGARET SSM
(Mother Superior, assumed office 6 March 1965)
Sister Columba
Sister Mary Joan

Obituaries
19 Jan 1999 — Sister Mary Thecla, aged 87, professed 43 years

Community Publication
Oremus, annually in Advent. Write to the Mother Superior. There is no fixed subscription, but donations towards stationery and postage are welcome.

Community History
Sister Catherine Louise SSM, *The Planting of the Lord: The History of the Society of Saint Margaret in England, Scotland & the USA;* privately published, 1995.

Guest and Retreat Facilities
There is one guest room available.

Most convenient time to telephone: 6.00 pm - 8.00 pm

Associates
There are a group of Associates.

Society of St Margaret

(Boston)

SSM

Founded 1855
(Boston Convent founded 1873)

St Margaret's Convent
17 Highland Park Street
Boston
MA 02119-1436
USA
Tel: 617 445 8961
Fax: 617 445 7120
E-Mail: ssmconvent@ssmbos.com
Website: ssmbos.com

Morning Prayer
6.00 am

Mass
7.30 am

Noon Office
12 noon

Evening Prayer
5.30 pm

Compline
8.30 pm

Office Book:
Book of Common Prayer of the Episcopal Church of the USA

St Margaret's Convent, Boston, is one of the five autonomous convents that compose the Society of St Margaret founded by John Mason Neale. The American Convent was established in 1873 to administer the Children's Hospital in Boston. Today, our mission is to the world around us and so it must cross all boundaries and respect the integrity of every other person. We find many institutions (hospitals, homes, schools, prisons, shelters, feeding programs and the Church) to be places where mission can take place. We also welcome into our houses individuals and groups who seek a place to pray or a place apart to plan and work. The essentials of our life are: Devotion to the Presence of Christ in the Holy Name, in the Blessed Sacrament, in our Sisters, in our neighbor and in Scripture. We are gathered in community, vowed to God, to one another and to the poor. We value one another and our diverse gifts. We have come together from many parts of the world as well as many places in the United States. There are others from Haiti, Tortolla, Trinidad, Jamaica, England and Canada.

Sister Adele Marie SSM (*priest*)
(*Mother Superior, assumed office March 1990*)
Sister Carolyn SSM (*Assistant Superior*)

Sister Joan
Sister Esther
Sister Marina Mary
Sister Bernardine
Sister Felicitas
Sister Lucy Mary
Sister Mary Christine
Sister Catherine Louise (*priest*)
Sister Jane Margaret
Sister Rosemary
Sister Marjorie Raphael
Sister Marion
Sister Virginia
Sister Mary Michael
Sister Emily Louise
Sister Mary Eleanor (*priest*)
Sister Gloria
Sister Marie Margaret
Sister Ann
Sister Claire Marie
Sister Katherine Mary
Sister Mary Gabriel
Sister Adele
Sister Julian
Sister Jennifer Anne
Sister Carolyn
Sister Christine
Sister Marie Therese
Sister Monica
Sister Brigid
Sister Elizabeth
Sister Promise

Novices: 4
Postulants: 1

Obituaries

7 Aug 1997 Sister Leslie Anne, aged 56, professed 30 years
7 Apr 1999 Sister Winifred, aged 91, professed 64 years

Addresses of other houses

St Margaret's Convent
Port-au-Prince
HAITI
Tel: 509 222 2011
Mailing address:
St Margaret's Convent, Port-au-Prince
c/o Agape Flights, Inc.
7990 15th Street East
Sarasota
FL 34243
USA

Neale House
50 Fulton Street
New York
NY 10038-1800
USA
Tel: 212 619 2672

St Margaret's House
5419 Germantown Avenue
Philadelphia
PA 19144-2223
USA
Tel: 215 844 9410

St Margaret's House
47 Jordan Road
New Hartford
NY 13413-2385
USA
Tel: 315 724 2324

Community Publication

St Margaret's Quarterly. For information, contact the Editor at the Boston Convent. The subscription rate is $5.

Community History

Sister Catherine Louise SSM, *The House of my Pilgrimage: a History of the American House of the Society of Margaret,* privately published, 1973.
Sister Catherine Louise SSM, *The Planting of the Lord: The History of the Society of Saint Margaret in England, Scotland & the USA;* privately published, 1995.

Community Wares

Haitian Gift Shop, with cards, crafts and altar linens for sale for the benefit of the Scholarship Fund for Holy Trinity School in Port-au-Prince. Available both at the Convent in Boston and in Port-au-Prince.

Guest and Retreat Facilities

All our houses have facilities for guests and retreatants. For costs and details of facilities, contact the house you are interested in.

Associates

Associates of one Convent of the Society of St Margaret are Associates of all. They have a common Rule, which is flexible to circumstances. They include men and women, lay and ordained. No Associate of the Society of St Margaret may be an Associate of any other Community.

Society of St Margaret

(East Grinstead)

SSM

Founded 1855

St Margaret's Convent
St John's Road
East Grinstead
West Sussex
RH19 3LE
UK

Tel: 01342 323497
Fax: 01342 328505

Matins
6.45 am
(7.30 am Sun,
7.20 am Thu)

Eucharist
7.20 am
(9.30 am Sun & Thu)

Litany of the Holy Name
8.25 am

Midday Office
12.45 pm

Vespers
5.05 pm (4.50 pm Sun)

Compline
8.35 pm

Office Book:
'A Community Office' printed for St Margaret's Convent, East Grinstead

Registered Charity:
No. 231926

Saint Margaret's Convent, East Grinstead, is one of the autonomous Houses which constitute the Society of St Margaret founded by John Mason Neale. The Sisters' work is the worship of God, expressed in their life of prayer and service. They welcome visitors to a guest house, a retreat house and a conference centre, Neale House, and are involved in spiritual direction, counselling and parish work. At Chiswick they care for elderly women in a nursing home and a guest house. There are two branch houses in Sri Lanka.

MOTHER RAPHAEL MARY SSM
(Mother Superior, assumed office 9 Feb 1985)
SISTER CYNTHIA CLARE SSM *(Assistant Superior)*

Sister Felicity
Sister Edna
Sister Rosemary
Sister Rosamond
Sister Winifred
Sister Hazel
Sister Sophia
Sister Lorna Mary
Sister Letitia
Sister Mary Joseph
Sister Mary Michael
Sister Rita Margaret
Sister Eleanor
Sister Jennifer Anne
Sister Lucy
Sister Barbara
Sister Mary Paul
Sister Elizabeth
Sister Mary Clare
Sister Sarah

Obituaries
3 Dec 1998 Sister Mary Joan, aged 95, professed 67 years

Other addresses
Neale House Conference Centre
Moat Road, East Grinstead, West Sussex RH19 3LB, UK
Tel & Fax: 01342 312552

St Mary's Convent & Nursing Home
Burlington Lane, Chiswick, London W4 2QF, UK
Tel: 0208 994 4641
Fax: 0208 995 9796

Community Publication
St Margaret's Chronicle, three times a year.

Write to the Editor at St Margaret's Convent.
£2.00 per annum, including p & p.

Community History

Sister Catherine Louise SSM, *The Planting of the Lord: The History of the Society of Saint Margaret in England, Scotland & the USA;* privately published, 1995.

Pamela Myers, *Building for the future: A Nursing History 1896 to 1996 to commemorate the centenary of St Mary's Convent and Nursing Home, Chiswick,* St Mary's Convent, Chiswick, 1996.

Doing the Impossible: a short sketch of St Margaret's Convent, East Grinstead 1855-1980, privately published, 1984.

Guest and Retreat Facilities

There are fourteen beds, primarily for individual retreats. Day retreatants are welcome both as individuals and in groups of up to twenty people. There are conducted Quiet Days once a month for up to twenty people. Some Sisters are available for support in these retreats. Donations appreciated.

Most convenient time to telephone: 10.00 am - 12 noon, 7.00 pm - 8.00 pm.

Associates

Associates observe a simple Rule, share in the life of prayer and dedication of the community, and are welcomed at all SSM convents.

SEMI-AUTONOMOUS HOUSES OVERSEAS

The Sisters run a Retreat House, a Children's Home (mainly for those orphaned in the ongoing civil strife), a Hostel for young women, a Home for elderly people, and are involved in parish work, church embroidery and wafer baking.

SISTER LUCY AGNES SSM
(Sister Superior, assumed office 1985)

Sister Edith
Sister Miriam
Sister Jane Margaret
Sister Maria Margaret
Sister Mary Christine
Sister Chandrani

St Margaret's Convent
157 St Michael's Road
Polwatte
Colombo 3
SRI LANKA

St John's Home
133 Galle Road
Moratuwa
SRI LANKA

Society of St Margaret

(Haggerston)

SSM

Founded 1855
(Haggerston Priory founded 1866)

St Saviour's Priory
18 Queensbridge Road
Haggerston
London
E2 8NS
UK
Tel: 0207 739 9976
(Revd Mother: 0207 739 6775)
Fax: 0207 739 1248
(The Sisters are not available on Mondays.)

Morning Prayer
7.15 am (8.00 am Sun)
followed by Eucharist
(12.15 pm Eucharist on major feasts & 12.30 pm on Sun)

Midday Office
12.45 pm

Evening Prayer
5.00 pm

Night Prayer
8.30 pm

Office Book:
Celebrating Common Prayer

Saint Saviour's Priory is one of the autonomous Houses which constitute the Society of St Margaret founded by John Mason Neale. The Community pursues the 'mixed' life of prayer and work, seeking to respond to some of the needs that arise in East London. The Office is four-fold and the Eucharist is offered daily. The Sisters' outreach to the local community includes: working as staff members in various parishes; supporting issues of justice and racial equality; working in schools and with young people; the homeless; those with HIV/AIDS; the sexually abused; retreats and individual spiritual direction. The Sisters are also called to a ministry of welcome: sharing their community building and resources of worship and space with individuals and groups.

SISTER ELIZABETH CRAWFORD SSM
(Revd Mother, assumed office February 1992)
SISTER ANNA HUSTON SSM *(Assistant Superior)*
Sister Natalie Bryan
Sister Beatrice Follows
Sister Susan Harris
Sister Pauline (Mary) Hardcastle
Sister Frances (Claire) Carter
Sister Joyce Anderson
Sister Marjorie Kelly
Sister Monica Popper
Sister Moira Jones
Sister Mary Michael (Lilian) Stokes
Sister Helen Loder *(priest)*
Sister Enid Margaret Jealous
Sister Pamela Radford
Sister June Atkinson
Sister Sue Makin
Sister Judith Blackburn

Novices: 2

Community Publication
The Orient, yearly. Write to The Orient Secretary at St Saviour's Priory. Brochures about the Community are available at any time on request.

Community Wares
Traidcraft, cards, books and religious items are all for sale.

Registered Charity: No. 230927

Madonna and Child

Sister Helen Loder SSM writes of the statue:

Maybe one of the greatest contributions made to the journey of Religious Life through the twentieth century has been Brother Roger of Taizé's emphasis on the value of the provisional. Daring gently to discard what no longer is appropriate is often balanced by reclaiming in a new way what once seemed to have lost its value. Part of this process for us has been the home, welcoming yet provisional, we have been able to offer to a seated Madonna and Child, with rabbits, made in 1925 by Mother Maribel CSMV (Wantage, UK), given to the CJGS sisters at West Ogwell, and now on long-term loan to us. Edwardian in style, with a hint of Peter Rabbit, yet determinedly contemporary child, she never fails to captivate our visitors by her mixture of tradition and realism. Yet again we feel we have arrived 'where we started and know the place for the first time' (T S Eliot, Little Gidding).

Community History

Memories of a Sister of S. Saviour's Priory, A.R. Mowbray, 1904.
A Hundred Years in Haggerston, published by St Saviour's Priory, 1966.
(*Both now out of print, but available for loan from St Saviour's Priory.*)

Sister Catherine Louise SSM, *The Planting of the Lord: The History of the Society of Saint Margaret in England, Scotland & the USA;* privately published, 1995.

Guest and Retreat Facilities

Six single and two double rooms for individual guests. Excellent facilities for non-residential group meetings.

Most convenient time to telephone: 10.30 am - 1.00 pm (Not Mondays).

Associates and Friends

Associates make a long term commitment to the Society of St Margaret, following a Rule of Life and helping the Community where possible. An Associate of one SSM house is an Associate of all the houses. There are regular quiet days for Associates who are kept in touch with community developments.

Friends of St Saviour's Priory commit themselves to a year of mutual support and friendship and are invited to regular events throughout the year.

Society of St Margaret

(Walsingham)

SSM

Founded 1855
(Walsingham Priory founded 1955)

The Priory of Our Lady
Walsingham
Norfolk
NR22 6ED
UK
Tel: 01328 820340
(Revd Mother)
Tel: 01328 820901
(Sisters & guests)
Fax: 01328 820899

Readings
& Morning Prayer
7.00 am (6.30 am Thu)

Mass
9.30 am
(7.15 am Thu,
10.00 am Sun)

Midday Office
12.45 pm

Vespers
5.00 pm

Compline
8.45 pm

Office Book:
The Divine Office

Registered Charity:
No. 255152

In January 1994, the Priory of Our Lady at Walsingham reverted to being an autonomous house of the Society of St Margaret. The Sisters' daily life is centred on the Eucharist and the daily Office, from which flows their growing involvement in the ministry of healing, and reconciliation in the Shrine, the local parishes and the wider Church. They welcome guests for short periods of rest, relaxation and retreat, and are available to pilgrims and visitors. They also work in the Education Department in the Shrine, Fakenham Surgery (Practice Nurse), volunteer work in the Sue Ryder Nursing Home, and in Falcon House, an ecumenical venture providing respite care for those with HIV/AIDS, and others marginalised by society.

MOTHER MARY TERESA SSM
(Revd Mother, assumed office 29 January 1994)

Sister Julian
Sister Joan Michael
Sister Christina Mary
Sister Mary Kathleen
Sister Alma Mary
Sister Jean Mary
Sister Francis Anne
Sister Wendy Renate
Sister Phyllis
Sister Jane Louise
Sister Sarah
Sister Sandra Luke

Postulants: 1

Community Publication
Community booklet to be published annually commencing July 1999. Write to The Priory for information.

Community History
Sister Catherine Louise SSM, *The Planting of the Lord: The History of the Society of Saint Margaret in England, Scotland & the USA;* privately published, 1995.

Community Wares
Cards (re-cycled) and embroidered; books; religious objects (statues etc.)

Guest and Retreat Facilities
Two single rooms in the Priory (women only). The Guest House at present is in process of major reconstruction. It is hoped that it will be available later in 2000 - for both men and women.

Most convenient time to telephone: 10.30 am - 12.30 pm; 2.30 pm - 4.30 pm; 6.30 pm - 8.30 pm.

Associates
There are associates and friends: for information apply to Revd Mother.

Society of St Paul

SSP

Founded 1958

PO Box 14350
Palm Desert
CA 92255-4350
USA

Tel: 760 568 2200

The Society of St Paul began in 1958 in Gresham, Oregon. Early ministry included nursing homes, a school, and commissary work in the Mid-East and Africa. In 1959, SSP was the first community for men to be recognized by the canons of the Episcopal Church in the United States.

Today, we perceive the call to become a community without walls, free to the movement of the spirit and not limited by ownership and responsibility of property or expectations of numerical strength. It shifts the focus from institutional life to ministry and prayer. We see ourselves embracing the whole Church as our community.

Reading the signs of profound change in the world and in the Church, we sense a new rôle for us as pilgrims and prophets. It requires a humble way of simplifying corporate life to be free to explore the emerging spirituality and ministry of the next century.

THE REVD BARNABAS HUNT SSP
(*Rector, assumed office 1989*)
THE REVD ANDREW RANK SSP (*Associate Rector*)

Community Publication
St Paul's Printer. Subscription is by donation. Contact Father Barnabas Hunt at the Palm Desert address.

Office Book:
Book of Common Prayer
of the Episcopal Church of the USA

Fellowship of St Paul
The Fellowship of St Paul, our extended family, is an association of Friends, Associates and Companions of The Society of St Paul, who live a Rule of Life centered on the Glory of God. Fellowship members support the Society and one another with their love, prayers and commitment. Fellowship members reflect the spirit of The Society of St Paul wherever they may be.

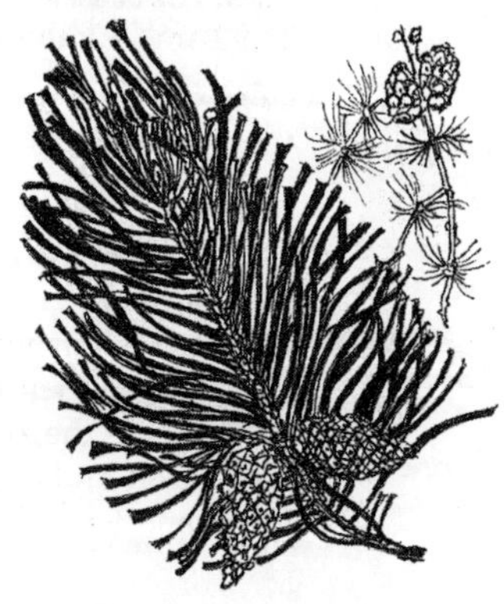

Society of the Sisters of Bethany

SSB

Founded 1866

*7 Nelson Road
Southsea
Hampshire
PO5 2AR
UK*

Tel: 023 92 833498

Mattins
7.00 am

Mass
7.45 am

Terce
9.00 am

Midday Office
12.00 noon

Vespers
5.00 pm

Compline
8.45 pm

Office book:
Anglican Office book with adaptations

Registered Charity:
No. 226582

By prayer and activity, the Sisters seek to share in the work of reconciling the divided Churches of Christendom and the whole world. By simplicity of life-style, the Sisters try to identify with those for whom they share in Christ's work of intercession in the power of the Holy Spirit. The work of the Sisters includes giving hospitality for those seeking spiritual or physical refreshment and arranging retreats and quiet days in their houses. They also extend their work to spiritual direction and helping in parishes. From time to time they are engaged in missions and cathedral chaplaincy work.

MOTHER GWENYTH SSB
(Revd Mother, assumed office 1 November 1994)
SISTER CHRISTINE ALICE SSB *(Assistant Superior)*

Sister Janet
Sister Margaret Faith
Sister Elisabeth Julian
Sister Christina Mary
Sister Margaret May
Sister Marjorie Mary
Sister Katherine Maryel
Sister Ruth Etheldreda
Sister Florence May
Sister Ann Patricia
Sister Constance Mary
Sister Hilary
Sister Mary Joy
Sister Rita-Elizabeth
Sister Teresa Mary

Novices: 1

Obituaries

12 Mar 1998 Sister Grace Ninian, aged 82, professed 48 years, Revd Mother 1974-84
14 Sep 1998 Sister Elspeth, aged 88, professed 40 years

Guest and Retreat Facilities

Four guest rooms. Individual retreatants can be accommodated.

Most convenient time to telephone:

10.00 am - 12 noon, 1.30 pm - 4.30 pm, 6.00 pm - 8.00 pm

Community Wares

Cards.

Associates

The associates are a body of close friends who unite their life of prayer to that of the community and who are accepted as members of an extended community family. They live in their own homes and accept a simple rule of life which is the expression of a shared concern to love and serve God and one another after the example of Martha, Mary and Lazarus.

Some other Religious Communities in the Anglican Communion

Key: ♂ men, ♀ women

AFRICA

♀ **Community of the Blessed Lady Mary** **(CBLM)**
Shearly Cripps Children's Home, PB600E, Harare, ZIMBABWE

♂ **Community of the Divine Compassion** **(CDC)**
St Augustine's Mission, PO Penhalonga, Mutare, ZIMBABWE

♀ ♂ **Chita Chezvipo Zvemoto** **(CCZ)**
(Community of the Gifts of the Holy Fire)
St Agnes Mission and Orphanage, Gokwe, ZIMBABWE

♀ **Community of the Holy Transfiguration** **(CHT)**
St David's Secondary School, P Bag T7904, Bonda Mission, Mutare, ZIMBABWE

♀ **Community of St John the Baptist** **(CSJB)**
PO Box 6, St Cuthbert's 5171, Eastern Cape, SOUTH AFRICA

♀ **Community of St Peter** **(CSP)**
PO Box 99, Hlatikulu, SWAZILAND

♀ **Sisterhood of St Paul** **(SSP)**
Maciene, MOZAMBIQUE

ASIA

♀ **Daughters of St Francis** **(DSF)**
Chung cheong bukdo Chopieong myen, Yeong jengri 483-12, KOREA

♀ **Order of St Benedict** **(OSB)**
810-1 Baekrok-ri, Habuk-myon, Yangsan-shi, Kyongnam-do, 626-860, KOREA
Tel: 51 523 841560

AUSTRALASIA & PACIFIC ISLANDS

♀ **The Clare Community** **(CC)**
Monastery of the BVM, Bucketts Way, Stroud, NSW 2425, AUSTRALIA
Tel: 2 4994 5303; Fax: 2 4994 5404

♀ **Community of the Sacred Name** **(CSN)**
181 Barbadoes Street, Christchurch 1, NEW ZEALAND *Tel: 3 366 8245*
40 Rintoul Street, Newton, Wellington, NEW ZEALAND *Tel: 4 389 4580*
St Christopher's Home, PO Box 8232, Nakasi, Suva, FIJI *Tel: 679 47 458*

EUROPE

♀ **Community of the Epiphany** **(CE)**
Copeland Court, Kenwyn, Truro, Cornwall TR1 3DR, UK

♀ **Society of the Franciscan Servants of Jesus and Mary** **(FSJM)**
Posbury St Francis, Crediton, Devon EX17 3QG, UK

♀ **Society of the Holy Trinity** **(SHT)**
Ascot Priory, Ascot, Berkshire SL5 8RT, UK

♀ **Society of Our Lady of the Isles** **(SOLI)**
Fetlar, Shetland Isles, UK

NORTH AMERICA & the CARIBBEAN

♀ **All Saints Sisters of the Poor** **(ASSP)**
All Saints' Convent, PO Box 3127, Catonsville, MD 21228, USA
Tel: 410 747 4104
Fax: 410 747 3321

St Anna's Home, 2016 Race Street, Philadelphia, PA 19103-1109, USA

♀ **Community of the Holy Spirit** **(CHS)**
St Hilda's House, 621 West 113th Street, New York, NY 10025-7916, USA
Tel: 212 666 8249
E-Mail: chs@interport.net

The Melrose Convent, Federal Hill Road, Brewster, NY 10509-9813, USA
Tel: 914 278 4854

♀ **Community of St Mary** ***(Southern Province)*** **(CSM)**
St Mary's Convent, 1100 St Mary's Lane, Sewannee, TN 37375 2614, USA
Tel & Fax: 931 598 0059
E-Mail: stmarys@seraphl.sewanee.edu

St Mary's Convent, 2619 Sagada, Mount Province, PHILIPPINES

St Mary's Convent, 5608 Monte Vista St, Los Angeles, CA 90042, USA
Tel: 213 256 5337

♀ **Order of St Anne** **(OSA)**
Convent of St Anne, 1125 North La Salle Street, Chicago, IL 60610, USA
Tel: 312 642 3638

♀ **Order of the Teachers of the Children of God** **(TCG)**
5870 East 14th Street, Tucson, AZ 85711, USA
Tel: 520 747 5280
Fax: 520 747 5236
E-Mail: smltcg@aol.com

Tuller School, Tuller Road, Fairfield, CT 06430, USA
Tel: 203 374 3636

Tuller School at Maycroft, PO Box 1991, Sag Harbour, NY 11963, USA
Tel: 516 725 1121

HIGH LEIGH
CONFERENCE CENTRE

Articles

Quiet Days in a Religious Community

by Christina Baxter

Why do I spend my Quiet Days at a Religious community house and not on top of a mountain or some other kind of place? That is the question, **Dr Christina Baxter,** *the Principal of St John's College, Nottingham, and a lay canon theologian of Coventry Cathedral, asked herself. Amidst her busy schedule, which includes not only the work of the College but also the responsibility of chairing the House of Laity of the General Synod, she regularly spends time with a Religious community. During such days, she has an opportunity for withdrawal and quiet. In this article, she explores her reasons for these Quiet Times and their significance in her life.*

How did it all begin?

As a young schoolteacher, I went on retreat to a convent with a group of people and found it helpful. Yet when I tried to spend a few days there alone, I left early. I had not understood what the time was for, nor was I ready for the silence and solitude.

A few years later, I joined the staff of St John's College. We started to spend our faculty Quiet Days with the Community of the Holy Cross at Rempstone, and keep one day each term when the whole College would keep a time of quiet. These Quiet Days were a new experience for me, and I was helped to make the most of them by the good teaching of my colleagues and by students. Yet, the experience was also partly familiar. As an Evangelical, I was used to keeping a 'quiet time' every day - the novelty was in extending it, and adding eating in silence and refraining from greeting people as one walked around. At the beginning, I did have to overcome a resentment within me about being made to be silent, and also counter my reluctance to use the whole time for God.

It was being elected to General Synod which prompted my occasional visits to the Convent to become a more regular part of my life. The experience of Synod increased my need to intercede by several incremental points. So I began to spend a whole day before each Synod praying for the agenda and my part in it. I was really struggling with the way in which other Anglicans on Synod were Christians, and so I was in urgent need of grace so as not to fall into the sins of hating, despising, ignoring or criticising them. Eventually, this led to the pattern of my taking one day a month, which I have now done for several years.

What are the characteristics of my times of quiet?

I never return from the Convent without knowing that I have been with God.

There are a range of ways by which this makes itself known. If I have a major decision to take, the quietness facilitates discernment, especially as I am in a place where I am surrounded by the loving prayers of the Sisters. When I have spent time in silent prayer, laying the possibilities and arguments before God, I discover a sense of what God wants me to do. I cannot tell you why I know, but I do. When I am invited to do something, I often say that I shall pray about it before I decide. I then take such requests with me on Quiet Days.

Dr Christina Baxter

Second, I sometimes go with sermons or retreats to prepare. Again, as I spend time with God and focus on Scripture, I find God speaking to me that 'I may speak in living echoes of his tone'. It is not that I am unaware of him on other occasions, but on Quiet Days it is like putting clothes into a drying machine - the natural processes are speeded up. So too, with listening to God: in silence I am in 'God's drier' and the process is speeded up!

Often I go with a great hunger for God or with a sense of tiredness or emptiness. I collapse into a rocking chair and God enfolds me in his love. He gently steals away my tiredness and fills me with the emotional and spiritual energy for the next steps on my journey.

Why the Convent and not my home?

There are many reasons why it is good to get away from home, but they are not to do with seeking silence as such, for, because I live alone, my home can also be a quiet place. I can be (and am) quiet with God at home. The problem there, however, is that I am surrounded by things which need to be done. Even though I confine my College work to my study at St John's, work of a different sort calls me at home, such as domestic chores and the lure of the garden. Plus, there is a temptation at home to rearrange my priorities, whereas a regular engagement in my diary to be away from home means I do not meddle with the time for quiet: it is fixed. Although, the pressures of work sometimes make it hard to keep the engagement with God, I now recognise that I do not get more work done by skipping the Quiet Day. In fact, I do achieve more after this day than I do at other times, because I return with the gift of mental and emotional energy.

Second, it is great to be unobtainable. At the Convent, no one can knock at my door or telephone me, and so I know that the time is absolutely set aside.

Third, I am able to join my prayers to those of the community. They have a pattern of daily prayer in which I can share, and this includes the Eucharist. The Quiet Day is a day in which I can pray without any responsibility for the pattern of psalms, intercession and praise. As I get older, the gift of being able to rest on the praying life of others becomes more and more significant to me. The Convent also ministers to me. In College, I am never 'off duty'. At Church, I am never beyond the reach of those in need. The Convent is one place where my own needs can emerge without fail. It is like a watering hole, where I do not have to hold back whilst others go before me to drink.

Fourth, the Convent is a place where my Sisters in Christ have undertaken to pray for me. I do many things in the course of a year. Having others intercede for me faithfully has been over the years, and still is, an enormous support: the Sisters are among this group. I am able to share with one of them, in confidence, matters which I am not at liberty to share elsewhere. There are times when it has been critical that I could have an intercessor to carry prayer requests for the ministry and responsibilities with which I am involved.

Religious give themselves to a life of prayer, which is a gift to the Church and to the world, and they allow us to share this. They can carry us to the Throne of Grace when we can not take ourselves there because we are too distracted by other matters. By their silent witness, they teach us more about silent prayer, sacrificial love, discipline, and about the God who calls us to daily acts of obedience.

At the Convent, I have learned ecumenical lessons too. I have been accepted, even though I do not share all the convictions the Sisters hold, or express my faith as they do. That has made it possible for me to accept them. And it has also been the wellspring for my understanding of many of my Anglican brothers and sisters whose life I do not very often encounter.

Can I recommend it to others?

I can and do suggest - often - that people take this kind of opportunity in a community near to wherever they find themselves. Perhaps the one word which sums it up is hospitality. In the generous hospitality of a community I find myself encountering God's gracious and generous hospitality, which is healing, life-giving and renewing.

The convent garden of the Society of the Holy Cross in Seoul, Korea

Kaire in Greece

by Sister Sue Makin SSM

Kaire is an interconfessional conference, mainly for women, which first met in 1971 and has since met every other year, in various locations. The participants are drawn together by the very fact that they are divided at the Eucharist. All are dedicated to serving the church, whether by monastic, priestly or diaconal vows, and so the gathering reflects a great variety of religious expression.

At the 1998 conference, held in August at Evangelistria in Greece, there were forty-two representatives from about a dozen countries. Here, ***Sister Sue SSM****, one of the Anglican participants, shares her reflections on a challenging week of ecumenical conversation.*

I had only a vague idea of what I was going to do. The Kaire conference was something I had heard about via CCC meetings. What a revelation I was in for! The conference was set in central Greece, high in the mountains, requiring a nail-biting twenty-minute ascent, with every bend a hairpin ... Sister Theodekti, our host, barely reassured us,

> 'It is good that your first experience of this road is in the dark. Tomorrow it will be light. If you are frightened, then close your eyes!'

This began a week full of surprises, not least because, for the entire week, nothing happened on time, leaving some of the English and German participants somewhat twitchy ... However, after the dismal English summer, I was very pleased to be where the sunshine was guaranteed.

The purpose of meeting together is not only to look at what divides the churches but also to explore the richness of traditions that are different to our own. Some differences may even be threatening. As a group, we try for one short week to understand where the other is coming from and to clarify the essentials of our own particular beliefs. I found this probably the most stimulating - and yet frustrating - aspect of the week. How do you explain the Church of England to a Greek Orthodox? How do you hold together the strands of Anglicanism in its glorious technicolour?

There was a genuine curiosity, and gracious reception, of what I had to say, even if it was in sign language! The evening before the Anglican Eucharist, Father Eric CR gave an excellent talk, a 'Beginners Guide to Anglicanism'. He was especially helpful in putting the Liturgy into context, even though he ran out of time on reaching the 1928 Prayer Book ... As there were only four Anglicans at the conference, I received much positive feedback and I felt that many myths were dispelled. In a sense, that is what we were there to do, to build an area of trust around the pain that seems to surround the wider Christian church.

Given the venue, the main input naturally came from the Greek Orthodox. Sister

Michaila gave a series of addresses entitled 'From crucifixion to resurrection', followed by pertinent questions for personal reflection. These addresses were both challenging to the Western ear, as well as being a window into the Orthodox way. Questions like: 'Do I experience the paradox of finding true life through giving up my will?', and 'Do I practise daily personal awareness of the need for the cross in my life? Does this awaken a sense of sin in me and spur me on to seek the remedy for this?' These were hard questions with which to grapple in our groups.

It seemed to me that even though our basis for faith is the same - that Jesus Christ is the Messiah, that he died and rose again for us - East and West seem to live out different aspects of this same story. My sense was that the Orthodox way can be summed up with a few of Sister Michaila's own words:

> 'Repentance begins with turning back to restore what was taken, to find what was lost,to undo what was done amiss ... Repentance is work.'

One of my main impressions of Orthodox Religious was the tremendous sense of industry to work out their repentance, to put things right by humility, prayer, fasting, loss of self, and above all obedience. In this way, they are a Good Friday people. This is not a negative comment. Undergirding this sense of repentance and pain of separation, there is a joy bubbling, a gentle but intense joy. It may possibly be a gross generalisation, but I think the church in the West is more an Easter people. In effect, we complete the whole by being who we are: we need each other.

The other main input from the Greek Orthodox was their generous hospitality. The warmth of the country was matched by the warmth of the people. One of the most moving experiences for me was visiting a newly-founded monastery at Thebes. There, on the top of the hill, was a breeze-block shell that was to be the sisters' living space. They are living in containers - literally, of the P & O variety - whilst it is built, relying on donations of materials. They were so happy to welcome us that they insisted on feeding us. These sisters have very little, their life is at the moment very hard, and yet what little they had they shared. Late that night we returned home, having celebrated with singing and being laden with gifts. Such generosity is very humbling.

We did a lot of eating, as each monastery we visited welcomed us with some form of food and drink, after the liturgy. Something I shall never forget was the sheer beauty of their churches, and of standing in front of frescoes which were a thousand years old, keenly aware of the depth of their heritage and the responsibility they carry both to preserve and to bring to life such ancient forms of worship. The singing of the Office has changed little in hundreds of years and was both haunting in its antiquity as it was striking in its robustness.

We also engaged in much talking, my group spending a lot of time wrestling with the Orthodox perspective. There were frank and sometimes heated exchanges, in various languages, and at these times we were a microcosm of the church at large, feeling the pain and struggle of misunderstanding - but we were talking and listening. The hope was that each member present could take some of the work done in these groups back to her own environment, even if it was merely promoting a greater tolerance amongst churches of differing traditions.

I certainly feel that I understand the Eastern Church in more depth and with less suspicion, even if I can not agree with some of their theological emphases. My only regret is that the conference did not hear much about the experience of other churches, but as an introduction of the Orthodox way it was invaluable. I hope too that the Orthodox representatives came to understand a little of the ministries of Religious in the West, and the different nature of bringing the Gospel to those around us.

I hope that this article gives a flavour of the work Kaire is doing and I would like to commend it to you. More dialogue needs to happen if the Christian Church is going to remain a force for good in an increasingly materialistic world. Its energy needs to be properly channelled. Fighting amongst ourselves is not a productive way of using the tremendous power of the Gospel. The energy must be positive. Kaire is a spark for that energy. I am grateful for the opportunity I was given to experience its dynamic, which has widened my perspective.

The symbol of Kaire is a mosaic. Mary Germani, in Kaire's magazine, described it in these words, which sum up the value of the conference,

> 'The beauty of the design depends on differences rather than uniformity of the parts. Kaire too attempts to gather the many expressions of Christian spirituality, and the distinctiveness of its members, into a pattern, that of a praying community which sees beyond.'

Reflections on being an Oblate, Tertiary, Companion or Associate

by Marion G. Fry

More and more people are responding to a vocation to be an Oblate or Tertiary of a Religious community. Many more are Companions and Associates. ***Dr Marion Fry****, herself a Companion of the Community of the Resurrection since 1963, here reflects on that vocation, how it comes about and what it means. Dr Fry lives for three months each year as an 'alongsider' with the Society of the Sacred Cross at Tymawr Convent in Wales, with the remainder of the year spent in her own home in Ontario, Canada.*

Those of us who are oblates, tertiaries, companions or associates of Anglican Religious communities live ordinary, secular lives of Christian faith and service. We may be ordained or lay, married or unmarried, young or old, male or female, working, out-of-work, or retired. We live in a restless, fast-moving world which continually challenges us to adapt to change, to show how competitive and productive we can be, and to be ready consumers of all the latest in material goods. Our world is restless, and so too are we. We are restless to the extent, firstly, that we are carried along by its strong currents, and, secondly, that human compassion and love of God bid us swim against these currents. In this latter restlessness, we are companions of all who value peace and justice above material possessions, and also of all who are searching, consciously or unconsciously, for God.

For many of us, it was an awakening of spiritual restlessness which led us to become oblates, tertiaries, companions or associates of our particular Religious communities. At first, there may only have been a rather vague longing for something 'more' than we were able to find in regular parish life, perhaps a 'deeper' approach to prayer or to Word and Sacrament. At some point, whether through a parish priest or someone else, each of us discovered that a certain convent or monastery had guest accommodation and also offered Quiet Days or Retreats. Then, there was a first visit. As we listened to an address, explored the book stall, let go of tensions in a silence which was surprisingly welcome, joined the community in worship, or talked for the first time with a member of the community, we were stirred by a sense of new possibilities to be explored. For each of us, it was by some such process that our vague spiritual longing for something 'more' began to find actual nourishment, through an as yet very informal association with a Religious community. Eventually, the possibility of formalizing that association emerged, like a vocation, summoning each of us to greater wholeness and depth of faith and life.

Coming to the point of making a formal commitment can be far from easy. We all live in a world which is increasingly unable to understand why anyone would make a long-term commitment. In a world changing as rapidly as ours, even the most loving human relationship is bound at times to experience strain, when, for example, work opportunities or career patterns change unexpectedly. In such a world, we are constantly reminded, flexibility is of paramount, practical importance. It is accordingly better to avoid 'tying yourself down' by making any long-term commitment; it is always preferable, we are told, to 'keep your options open'. No wonder then that making any long-term commitment can seem like swimming against the tide. In such a climate, formalizing a link with a Religious community on a long-term - or even lifetime - basis requires particularly strong and clear-eyed motivation. Many of us can testify that that kind of motivation emerges with a persistent sense of vocation, a sense of being called by name to undertake such a commitment. Formed in response to the initiative of God, it comes as a gift of grace. Our spiritual restlessness has actually been given a sense of direction which it proposes to follow.

The commitment is not, however, one-sided, nor is the process leading up to it one-sided. The formal commitment must seem right to the community concerned as well as to the individual. Once the question of formal affiliation has been raised, there needs to be time and opportunity for this discernment. When this process results in the formal admission of an oblate, tertiary, companion or associate at the end of the probationary period, then both parties are committed to supporting one another through prayer, whilst sharing the same governing intention. Most fundamentally, it is that sharing of intention between members of the community and those formally linked with it which shapes the extended family of any community. Shared intention is its *raison d'être,* mutual prayer its bonding.

We all know that the shared intention is lived according to a Rule. While most people in our society will be aware that members of Religious communities observe Rules, they would find it very difficult to understand why anyone living an ordinary, secular life would formally undertake to do so. No one thinks that it is necessary to be 'tied down' to a Rule in order to live a Christian life, and most would

SSF tertiaries at the Third Order Diamond Jubilee gathering in 1996

think it is undesirable, given the need we all have to be able to move with the times. As contemporary oblates, tertiaries, companions and associates, we are all aware of this line of thought. Indeed, most of us can find echoes of it in our own minds, and for that reason we need to address it.

Have we tied ourselves up in a way that is undesirable? There is a catch in the question, assuming as it seems to do that by undertaking our Rules we are sacrificing freedom and flexibility. Yet consider our Rules. They do not prescribe uniform practice for us all, regardless of our personal circumstances or regardless of where we are on our spiritual journeys. Even a seeming 'invariable' in a Rule, such as weekly or more frequent attendance at the Eucharist, usually carries the proviso, 'whenever possible'. Most Rules, moreover, include 'variables', for example, prescriptions for spiritual reading, prayer and service, which expressly require to be adapted to the individuals concerned and not only initially, when the rule is first undertaken, but over the years. Normally such adaptations are made in consultation with the Religious community concerned. In short, our Rules are not in themselves inflexible. We have tied ourselves down to following Rules-as-interpreted-in-consultation.

Still, the question may be pressed. Why do we tie ourselves down to a Rule? Our answer can only come from reflection on our experience of actually observing our Rules over the years. Most of us want to say that the rhythm and regularity of observance is genuinely supportive and helpful; in that it is like a good friend, and it is also like a good habit. Over the years, the rhythm and pattern is moreover spiritually nourishing, as our spiritual restlessness is steadied by being focussed on the love of God. Faithful observance of our Rules right through desolate or troubled times really does mature our faith. Every so often we realize that we have moved into a different place in relation to God, in short, that we have grown spiritually. And very occasionally, we are sure that faithful observance of our Rules has by God's grace brought us to the threshold of some far-reaching change in our spiritual lives. It may be that we are at last ready to let go of some personal 'idol', having painfully acknowledged that it is an 'idol'; or it may be that we are ready for some new form of prayer or of service. At such moments, we know that we are free to change, indeed ready for it. We are very keenly aware that the grace of God has been partner with us in bringing the observance of our Rules and by it our spiritual journey to a landmark point.

In conclusion, three observations seem to be in order. The first is that the longer we have lived faithfully according to our Rules, the better able we are to testify to the nourishing and liberating effect it has over all. That is partly because spiritual growth takes time, and partly because we can be wiser by hindsight. The second observation is that it is very important to review, at least annually, the 'spirit' of our Rules, that statement of the intention which we share with all others who are formally linked with our respective communities, and also with the members of those communities. It is there that we are reminded that we have committed ourselves for a purpose which motivates our lives. The third and final observation is that, geographical separation notwithstanding, we do not observe our Rules as isolated individuals, but as members of extended community families in the context of that mutual support and very real companionship of prayer. For that, we all have very good reason to be thankful.

The Meaning of the Vow of Poverty in the Developing World

by Richard Carter

Poverty is the experience of so many people living in the developing world. So what is the meaning of the Religious vow of poverty in such a context? ***Father Richard Carter*** *is a priest from Britain working in the Solomon Islands, chaplain to the Melanesian Brotherhood, the largest Anglican Religious community in the world. He reflects here on the vow of poverty as seen from a Melanesian perspective.*

For many young people in Melanesia, to enter a Religious community is an enviable opportunity. The waiting lists are full. The Melanesian Brotherhood has one hundred and twenty novices, and each year many are turned down owing to lack of accommodation or insufficient resources. The Religious communities provide a way out of the village; a training for those who may have been deprived of post-primary school education, a chance to travel and to broaden experience. Above all, joining a Religious community provides a sense of purpose. A dedicated brother or sister will be greatly respected, spoken of with pride by their families and villages as one they have given to serve God. So, if the Religious communities are providing increased opportunity and status for their members where does the vow of poverty fit into all of this?

Like Religious Life anywhere in the world, the motives for becoming a brother or sister are mixed. In Melanesia, those who come simply for self-advancement, and do not grow beyond that stage, will not stay long. The opportunities that arise do not negate the vow of poverty, but are part of the blessings and possibilities which God opens up for those who are called - for there will certainly be many sacrifices and difficulties to overcome. For at its heart, the vow of poverty is a calling as much in the developing world as it is in the West. The temptations to become acquisitive and grasping - or plain disillusioned - are just as pervasive.

For, alongside all the joy which is the character of community life in Melanesia, the vow of poverty will be something with which each brother will have to struggle sooner or later. Even before they come to the community, they know this. The founder of the Melanesian Brotherhood believed that the standard of life of the community must never rise above those they wish to serve. The brothers, he believed, must be prepared to share the lives, homes, work and food of everyone. Again and again, I have seen that it is this ability to share without prejudice or judgement that makes the brothers so welcome.

Within their own community, resources are limited. For example, more than forty novices share each humid dormitory, sleeping on mats. They have no shoes and no watches. They own a few tattered clothes, usually passed from one to another, or novice uniforms. Towels are usually shared and threadbare. Most have no 'luxuries', such as razor blades, soap, washing powder or toothpaste. (These will sometimes be given as gifts.) Most can fit their possessions into one bag. The community eats twice a day: root crops and some vegetables. Sometimes there will be a little fish. In the bush areas, they can usually find fruit and always there are coconuts. At times, there will be feast days, pigs will be killed and major fishing expeditions will go out: then there will be plenty. At other times, when the floods and rains come, there may be only potatoes or even nothing. The days when there is no evening meal, the brothers call 'find your own way home'. It means everyone must fend for themselves or simply go to bed.

The brothers aim to take special care of any guest who arrives at the community, and so will therefore hold back to make sure all others are properly fed before themselves. Portions are divided, and divided again, as guests arrive. Often you will notice those who quietly go without and this is done with no resentment at all. The community are not advocating deprivation: neither is it glorifying in a spirit of fasting. (When there is plenty, the community will eat as if there is no tomorrow.) Yet the brothers will tell you there is freedom in this way of life, this lack of grasping. A freedom to accept what the day provides and to embrace both the feast and the famine. The Head Brother said to me,

> "It is good that sometimes I learn to go without. We cannot always have what we want and this way I learn to appreciate what I do have."

It can also lead to a greater awareness of the needs of others.

The vow of poverty is not only about sharing but is also about with whom you share. A mark of a Christ-centred community is that it will have a special love and concern for those who Christ embraced: especially the lost, the sick and the rejected. And one's own experience of need will become the source of one's relationship and empathy with others. This will require a brave reaching out beyond the confines of one's culture to those who have been rejected by that same culture.

An old man died near the village of Vila. He was a lonely man who had arrived from the weather coast, on the other side of the island, with no family with him. The village was suspicious of him and the children frightened. High grass was growing around his home and he never seemed to eat or wash. For some reason or problem, he had been rejected by his own community and now the Melanesian Brothers were his only visitors. When he was found dead in the grass by his house, no one would touch him. He had been sick - perhaps they would get sick too? They called two novices, who carried him back to his home, washing and cleaning his body and prepared him for burial, wrapped in a bed sheet. In the evening, more Melanesian brothers and novices arrived, and prayed and sang around his body through the night. The villagers, no longer afraid, came and joined them. In the morning, the body of the old man was buried. A lonely death - but one transformed: now embraced by the love of God.

Perhaps one of the great benefits of this vow of poverty is the way it can bring out all that is best and most generous in others. Among a people who are often divided and suspicious of people from other tribes and islands, this Brotherhood can cut across the barriers. The brothers can and do become part of the extended family of any community, irrespective of tribe or language. I have seen this even among our brothers working as far away as the Philippines or those who have visited the UK. Everyone knows they have nothing and it seems to release a wonderful generosity of spirit; they can become the sons of everyone. The poorest of villagers themselves can become the hosts and the greatest generosity and joy is often found at the homes of those who have least, for all need an opportunity to give. One of the greatest deprivations is surely to feel ashamed to offer, for fear that it will not be fit. Families will talk with joy about the way the brothers or sisters came and visited or stayed with them and often there is a real sense that this visiting, this sharing has brought a touch of Christ.

Part of this vow of poverty is also a generosity of time. The western world has sadly lost the meaning of this, where every moment, including leisure time, must be planned and made accountable. In the developing world, people and relationships are nearly always more important than one's own plans and programmes. Part of the life of poverty will be being open and ready for others when they come, however inconvenient, and being willing to respond to the needs of others. I sent a message to the Sisters of Melanesia asking to borrow a book from their library. The following morning, two sisters arrived at my house for breakfast. They had walked fifteen miles to bring the book. This kind of action is not rare. An old woman arrives at our community claiming that someone has harvested her garden and stolen her produce. She asks that the brothers pray that the thief will be caught. Instead, a group of brothers go with her to make a new garden. Wherever you walk or work or pray, there are people willing to walk, work or pray with you. Is this not a need everywhere in the world? I remember as a child the greatest thing about going to the Franciscans at Hilfield Friary in Dorset (UK) was that there the brothers had time for you: an availability, to walk, to talk, to pray and to share without

the sense that there were much more important things that they should be doing.

When you walk up a mountain path on the weather coast of Guadalcanal and the way grows more treacherous and the drop more sheer, so too, unobtrusively, grows the support of the brothers who walk with you: guiding, carrying bags, and at exactly the right time supporting you to prevent a fall. It is a rare gift, an acute awareness of the needs of the present moment, without any sense of judgement. It is our clinging to independence and our failure to trust which becomes our death. A Religious community may seem poor, but they make many rich, for knowledge and skill and time are not a private possession but there to be shared by all.

The community at Tabalia is preparing for the Brotherhood feast day of St Simon and St Jude. For two weeks, people have been arriving from every part of the Solomons to join the celebration. The brothers and novices have vacated their rooms and dormitories; these will be for the visitors and they themselves will sleep anywhere they can find - verandahs, sheds, even down at the piggery. More than 5,000 people will arrive in time for the weekend of the feast day. The taps dry up. No one complains; water is carried half a mile from the river. No one is bossing, no one is shouting; there is an atmosphere of joy and celebration. The community is working together with a harmony that remains a mystery to the overseas guests. No one pays, no one is quite sure where it has all come from or who is feeding whom, but, like the feeding of the 5,000, again and again there is enough for everybody. It is a miracle of reciprocity.

Poverty is also about living by faith. It has become a joke among the brothers:

"Have you eaten today?"

"Not yet, I am living by faith."

The vow does bring deep awareness of God in all things. There is an awareness of dependence on God in the storms, floods and cyclones, which can so easily destroy people's livelihoods and homes. There is a deep awareness of God as brothers set off by canoe for other islands or to fish in rough seas. There is a constant awareness of God in creation. When the rainy season comes, the taps silt up and there is thick mud everywhere. The brown swollen river, which can move bridges, is the only place to wash. There is a prayer on the lips of most brothers as two by two they walk the hot roads with bare feet and hope that a truck will stop to give them a lift. And yet no brother will look back or hold out his hand to stop anyone - all goodness must be freely given. There is a faith too as a brother with little formal education gets up to preach in a church or teach in a school or kneel down at the bed of the sick to pray for healing.

Poverty in the West is discussed in a very human context of contrasting one person with another, and assessed in terms of profession, income and property. In the developing world, God cannot be taken out of the equation so easily. A brother may be poor in material possessions but in Christ he is seen as rich. Life is seen as a gift of God. Ultimately, in Melanesia, at the decisive moments of life, the one who can intercede with God is needed more than the rich man with his worldly wealth. For all those who live in the developing world know the vulnerability and fragility of human life. They have all witnessed death in their community and have seen and mourned for those of all ages whom God has called to return to the creator. For those who know the poverty of death and do not try to hide it from their young, it is far wiser to prepare for eternity than concentrate on material things which will be taken away. Perhaps it is the western world which is really living in poverty, failing to see life as a gift - instead seeing it as a private possession. Thus in death, they are cheated and lose, whereas in Melanesia they are never parted.

The vow of poverty is not advocating a spiritual materialism: the storing up of treasure in heaven because one wants to be rich there. Rather it is a realisation of what those true treasures are. It is the miracle of love by which the more love is given for another, the more that love is also returned to bless the one who gives:

... by purity, knowledge, patience, holiness of spirit, genuine love, truthful speech, and the power of God; with the weapons of righteousness for the right hand and for the left; in honour and dishonour, in ill repute and good repute. We are treated as imposters, and yet are true; as unknown, and yet are well-known; as dying, and see - we are alive; as punished, and yet not killed; as sorrowful, yet always rejoicing; as poor, yet making many rich; as having nothing, and yet possessing everything. (2 Corinthians 5, 6-10).

At its best, the vow of poverty is transfigured into a vow of blessing in which there is great freedom. This is a message so at odds with the prescribed wisdom of our consumerist world that we have often abandoned or downplayed its radical demands. Is it possible to live this vow again, not only in the developing world but in the rest of the world? And why do I, who have witnessed this truth, still shrink from it? It is because, as with many of us, I fear the powerlessness of having no money and no escape. I fear being cut off from my family. I am concerned about hunger and sickness, and becoming a burden; being unable to get out if the going gets tough and missing the luxuries at the end of the hard journey. I wonder whether I would not feel vulnerable and trapped, oppressed by poor leadership, dispossessed, even exploited or forgotten: no longer in control but controlled. For this is also the experience of poverty in the developing world. And yet I deeply long for the freedom of that vow; the freedom of those I have seen coming so uncluttered to God, ready to serve him and their neighbour in all things; a poverty where service for others becomes pure grace; where everyone can become your brother, your sister, your mother. Can this vision of Christlike poverty be true? And quietly, humbly, the brothers and sisters who embrace this call seem to say: "Live the Gospel and you will see".

Anglican Religious

by Petà Dunstan

Religious Life among Anglicans has usually been seen as a development of the Victorian era. However, in this article, ***Dr Petà Dunstan****, a Fellow of St Edmund's College in the University of Cambridge (England), considers the Religious communities of the 1840s in a wider perspective. She explores the idea that Religious Life is latent in all Christian communities and therefore Anglicans should not define Religious Life only in the terms of their own nineteenth-century revival.*

A few years ago, I gave a talk at my college in Cambridge on the subject of Religious Life among Anglicans. It was to a small group of interested academics and, at the end, we had a question-and-answer session. The audience included a distinguished American Roman Catholic nun, who was on sabbatical with us, and her question took me by surprise: with there having been fewer vocations in the past thirty years, did I think Anglican Religious Life would survive? Without a moment's hesitation, I found myself answering a confident yes.

Reflecting later on the exchange, I realized that this strong conviction was connected to my historical perspective. For to me, the Church and Religious Life are intimately connected. It is never the presence of Religious Life which should surprise or need explanation but its absence. The impulse to Religious Life is endemic among Christians. It is merely the forms and expressions of it which differ in various historical situations. I would contend that only particular expressions of the vocation die out. The call itself is ever present.

In looking at the Anglican Communion, this means therefore leaving behind the idea that Religious Life 'began' in the 1840s. It is true that the Oxford Movement, from 1833, provided a theological perspective and dynamic in the Church of England which gave many the confidence to found Religious communities in its wake. These communities were a particular response to the social and religious situation in which they found themselves. The Religious wore the clothes appropriate to their time and developed patterns of life conducive to success in their own era. (Those that did not soon faded away.) Their work was heroic and the success of all they did, particularly pioneering in health and education and social projects, is seen in the fact that so much of what they did has now been taken over by the state. Communities showed the need: society then responded. This was prophetic work.

Ironically however, the very achievements of these communities meant that they themselves would no longer be needed in the same specific form. The fall in vocations in nursing and teaching orders from the First World War onwards was a reflection of this. The decline was a sign of tasks successfully completed. Yet, for those who associated Religious Life with those particular jobs and institutions, and with the wearing of particular habits, this decline was painfully interpreted as a decline in Religious Life itself. Many have felt diminished and despairing as once flourishing orders have been reduced to a handful of members and some communities have died altogether. Seen exclusively from the view of the past one hundred and fifty years of the Church of England, the statistical decline might be interpreted as marking the 'end' of the movement.

Yet seen from a wider historical perspective, going back to the early centuries of the Church, the rise and fall of specific communities and specific works is part of the rhythmic cycle of Religious Life. The spark is lit and burns brightly, only to die down in another generation, before re-emerging, perhaps in a different form, in another time. Even the Reformation, with its staunch and emotive propaganda against the vowed life, did not destroy the possibility of Religious Life forever. There are now monks and nuns in the churches which are the direct spiritual descendents of Martin Luther.

For Anglican Religious Life, the passing of some communities founded in the Victorian era is not therefore the end of a story. It should be remembered that from the 1540s to the 1840s, when in the Church of England vowed Religious seemed only a remote echo from the past, the values - and sometimes corporate traditions - of Religious Life nevertheless survived under many guises. One example was within College chapels in Oxford and Cambridge, which remained distinctly Benedictine in ethos and arrangement of worship. Fellows of Colleges even had to resign if they married, a custom which continued until the second half of the nineteenth century. Similarly, some traditions of cathedrals remained intertwined with the patterns of Religious Life. Amongst some families, the idea of community took hold, most notably that of Nicholas Ferrar at Little Gidding; where the family and household gathered daily to say the Office together. Yet again, there were alms houses where all those admitted became 'brothers' and wore a distinctive 'habit'. Similar observations might be made regarding hospices and the care of the sick, and also with respect to some missionary movements. The Reformation had banished the communities - but not the call to live out their values.

The explanation for this is simple. Religious Life is not an added extra to the Church, but rather it is at its heart. For Religious Life is nothing more nor less than the living out of Christian values - but in a particular and intense form. The desire to seek God, to study the scriptures, to practise Christian virtues through community life and to serve the poor and needy in the world - these are all aims of the *Christian* life. The vows and traditions of Religious are a means of pursuing these goals from a position beyond the conflicting responsibilities that can arise from wealth, marriage and children, and power. But the aim is essentially the same seeking of God that is the heart of any Christian witness. Religious Life, therefore, does not belong to any one denomination or part of the Church, but is a resource, an impulse, a potential for any faith community rooted in the Christian gospel.

The consequences of this perspective for Anglican communities are important. First, they have a much longer and broader tradition to draw upon than the patterns which inspired the pioneers of the 1840s revival. The founders and foundresses of the last century have much still to teach but they are only a part of the riches available for Anglican Religious as they enter the twenty-first century. The writings of the early monks and nuns and their way of life are the inheritance of all Religious, whatever denomination they belong to.

This is emphasized by the fact that in the past few decades, Anglican Religious have finally been able to disassociate themselves from the Victorian controversies over churchmanship, so bitter and divisive, of which they were seen by many as a symbol. The days when monks and nuns were seen as part of the partisan army of an Anglo-Catholic party fighting for recognition are now gone. Some of today's Religious are from Evangelical church backgrounds, in which fifty years ago a conventional Religious vocation would have been unthinkable. Equally, others come from non-church-going families, for whom the old ecclesiastical battles have no meaning in their own Christian journey.

Second, if Religious Life is a universal call then the ecumenical implications are immense. For Religious, the opportunities for building bridges between denominations are strong. The presence of Religious in the Anglican Communion is in itself an ecumenical witness, to which the Archbishop of Canterbury attested in his Foreword to the 1999 *Year Book*. This is because, for many churches, the presence of Religious Life is a sign of the depth of another church's spirituality and way of life. The late Father Pedro Arrupe SJ drew out the full ecumenical implications of this when he said that the vows of Religious transcended denomination. They created a unity between Religious of different churches which was of more significance than all that divided them. Religious can be a part of what brings the Christian family together if this truth is fully understood.

Finally, the historical view of Religious Life can only be a source of confidence for all Religious, even those whose communities may seem frail. For at many times in the long unfolding of the Church's journey, communities have suffered loss - and sometimes persecution - and yet their values have survived. As one community fades away, another is born, perhaps in a different part of the world. When First Order vocations are down, Third Order numbers may be rising. One has only to think of the pressures on the early monks and nuns, such as for the hermits of the desert, or the women of Rome - in the face of ridicule - making their homes into Religious houses, to understand the strength of the vocation. Many Religious in the developing world face the same threats today of war and upheaval, hostile governments and conflicts. In the West, dangers such as secularization, indifference to religion, and the lack of commitment that can arise from an over-emphasized individualism are every bit as threatening, even if in a different way. Yet, the values of Religious Life are not destroyed. The need for them is instead made more clear.

This is not to say that particular expressions of Religious Life will all survive. An attachment to externals can be a problem for some communities: a style of dress, a pattern of customs, a particular work, an institution, or a set of buildings. All these may not survive, but their disappearance would not signal the end of Religious Life. The Cluniac Benedictines, a well-known order of the medieval period, died out and yet their demise did not mean the end of the Benedictine witness. Similarly, the seed of Religious Life proved so embedded among Anglicans that even three hundred years of suppression could not eventually stop communities being formed again, once conditions allowed.

That is why I had such confidence to answer in the affirmative when asked the question with which I began this article. Even if sociology and other academic disciplines are not always encouraging to Religious, the witness of history has something different to say.

Glossary and Indices

GLOSSARY

Aspirant
A person who hopes to become a Religious and has been in touch with a particular community, but has not yet begun to live with them.

Celibacy
The commitment to remain unmarried and to refrain from sexual relationships. It is part of the vow of chastity traditionally taken by Religious. Chastity is a commitment to sexual integrity, a term applicable to fidelity in marriage as well as to celibacy in Religious Life.

Chapter
The council or meeting of Religious to deliberate and make decisions about the community. In some orders, this may consist of all the professed members of the community; in others, the Chapter is a group of members elected by the community as a whole to be their representatives.

Clothing
The ceremony in which a postulant of a community formally becomes a novice, and begins the period of formation in the mind, work and spirit of the community. It follows the initial stage of being a postulant when the prospective member first lives alongside the community. The clothing or novicing ceremony is characterised by the Religious 'receiving' the habit, or common attire, of the community.

Contemplative
A Religious whose life is concentrated on prayer inside the monastery or convent rather than on social work or ministry outside the house. Some communities were founded with the specific intention of leading a contemplative lifestyle together. Others may have a single member or small group living such a vocation within a larger community oriented to outside work.

Enclosed
This term is applied to Religious who stay within a particular convent or monastery - the 'enclosure' - to pursue more effectively a life of prayer. They would usually only leave the enclosure for medical treatment or other exceptional reasons. This rule is intended to help the enclosed Religious be more easily protected from the distractions and attentions of the outside world.

Eremitic
The eremitic Religious is one who lives the life of a hermit, that is, largely on his or her own. Hermits usually live singly, but may live in an eremitic community, where they meet together for prayer on some occasions during each day.

Evangelical Counsels
A collective name for the three vows of poverty, chastity and obedience.

Habit
The distinctive clothing of a community. In some communities, the habit is worn at all times, in others only at certain times or for certain activities. In some communities, the habit is rarely worn, except perhaps for formal occasions.

Novice
A member of a community who is in the formation stage of the Religious Life, when she or he learns the mind, work and spirit of the particular community whilst living among its members.

Oblate
Someone associated closely with a community, but who will be living a modified form of the Rule, which allows him or her to live outside the Religious house. Oblates are so-called because they make an oblation (or offering) of obedience to the community instead of taking the profession vows. In some communities, oblates remain celibate, in others they are allowed to be married. A few oblates live within a community house and then they are usually termed intern(al) oblates. The term oblate is more usually associated with Benedictine communities.

Office/Daily Office/Divine Office
The round of liturgical services of prayer and worship, which mark the rhythm of the daily routine in Religious Life. Religious communities may use the services laid down by the Church or may have their own particular Office book. The Offices may be called Morning, Midday, Evening and Night Prayer, or may be referred to by their more traditional names, such as Mattins, Lauds, Terce, Sext, None, Vespers and Compline.

Postulant
Someone who is in the first stage of living the Religious Life. The postulancy usually begins when the aspirant begins to live in community and ends when he or she becomes a novice and 'receives the habit'. Postulants sometimes wear a distinctive dress or else may wear secular clothes.

Profession
The ceremony at which a Religious makes promises (or vows) to live the Religious Life with integrity and fidelity to the Rule. The profession of these vows may be for a limited period or for life. The usual pattern is to make a 'first' or simple profession in which the vows are made to the community. After three or more years a Life Profession may be made, which is to the Church and so the vows are usually received by a bishop. In the Anglican Communion, Life Professed Religious can usually be secularised only by the Archbishop or Presiding Bishop of a Province.

Religious
The general term for a person living the Religious Life, whether monk, nun, friar, brother, sister etc.

Rule
The written text containing the principles and values by which the members of a community try to live. The Rule is not simply a set of regulations, although it may contain such, but is an attempt to capture the spirit and charism of a community in written form. Some communities follow traditional Rules, such as those of St Benedict or St Augustine, others have written their own.

Tertiary/Third Order
This term is usually associated with Franciscan communities, but is used by others

too. A Third Order is made up of tertiaries, people who take vows, but modified so that they are able to live in their own homes and have their own jobs. They may also marry and have children. They have a Rule of Life and are linked to other tertiaries through regular meetings. In the Franciscan family, the Third Order complements both the First Order of celibate friars and sisters and the Second Order of contemplative Religious.

Vows
The promises made by a Religious at profession. They may be poverty, chastity and obedience. In some communities, they are obedience, stability and conversion of life.

Index of Communities by Dedication or Patron Saint

Index of Communities by Location

AUSTRALIA

BANGLADESH

CANADA

DOMINICAN REPUBLIC

FRANCE

FIJI

USA

Index of Communities by Initials

Index of Community Wares & Services for Sale

Look up the item or service you require and then contact the communities listed for more information. Their addresses can be found in the Directory section.

AGRICULTURAL & FARM PRODUCTS

ALTAR BREAD

BOOKS, PAMPHLETS & LEAFLETS

CALENDARS

CALLIGRAPHY

CANDLES

CARDS

CD-ROMs

ıEEDLEWORK, EMBROIDERY & VESTMENTS

RAFTS

ICONS / ICON PRINTS

INCENSE

JAMS & PRESERVES

PRINTING